The Wedding Between Nero and Sporo: A Historical Love Story

Copyright Page

TITLE: The Wedding Between Nero and Sporo: A Historical Love Story

1ST Edition

Copyright @ 2023

ISBN: 9798223832836

Table of Contents

Title Page 1

The Wedding Between Nero and Sporo: A Historical Love Story 6

Chapter 1: The Wedding Between Nero and Sporo: A Historical Love Story...7

Chapter 2: Wedding Planning for Historical Themed Weddings......... 12

Chapter 3: Historical Reenactment Weddings 20

Chapter 4: Roman Empire-inspired Wedding Themes 27

Chapter 5: LGBTQ+ Historical Weddings.................................... 34

Chapter 6: Unique Wedding Venues for Historical Enthusiasts 41

Chapter 7: Ancient Roman Wedding Traditions and Rituals................ 46

Chapter 8: Historical Wedding Attire and Fashion 53

Chapter 9: Historical Wedding Photography and Videography........... 60

Chapter 10: Historical Wedding Favors and Decorations...................... 66

Chapter 11: Wedding Reception Entertainment with a Historical Twist 73

The Wedding Between Nero and Sporo: A Historical Love Story

By Roberto Miguel Rodriguez

Chapter 1: The Wedding Between Nero and Sporo: A Historical Love Story

Introduction to Nero and Sporo's Relationship

In the annals of history, few love stories have captured the imagination quite like that of Nero and Sporo. Their union, often seen as a symbol of forbidden love, transcended societal norms and left an indelible mark on the ancient Roman Empire. This subchapter delves into the captivating tale of Nero and Sporo's relationship, exploring the depths of their love and the challenges they faced in a society bound by tradition.

As historians, we have the privilege of uncovering the truth behind this historical romance, piecing together fragments of their lives to paint a vivid picture of their unique love story. From the early days of their courtship to their grand wedding ceremony, every aspect of Nero and Sporo's relationship is a testament to their unwavering love and their defiance of societal expectations.

"The Wedding Between Nero and Sporo: A Historical Love Story" not only explores the personal aspects of their relationship but also provides valuable insights for those interested in historical-themed weddings. Wedding planning for historical enthusiasts can draw inspiration from Nero and Sporo's union, incorporating elements of Roman Empire-inspired themes, LGBTQ+ historical weddings, and ancient Roman traditions and rituals.

For those seeking unique wedding venues, imagine exchanging vows in a grand amphitheater reminiscent of ancient Rome or a picturesque villa adorned with classical Roman architecture. The book also offers guidance on historical wedding attire and fashion, showcasing the opulent garments Nero and Sporo donned on their special day.

Capturing the essence of a historical wedding requires exceptional photography and videography skills. In this subchapter, we explore the techniques used to bring these cherished moments to life, ensuring that every frame reflects the grandeur and emotion of the occasion.

Moreover, the chapter details historical wedding favors and decorations, providing readers with inspiration for creating an ambiance that transports guests to a bygone era. From intricate Roman-inspired centerpieces to personalized tokens reminiscent of ancient Rome, these ideas infuse a historical twist into the smallest details.

Finally, no historical-themed wedding would be complete without captivating entertainment. Whether it's classical musicians, period actors, or even a reenactment of Nero and Sporo's love story, this subchapter offers unique ideas to ensure a wedding reception that will leave guests enthralled.

In conclusion, the subchapter "Introduction to Nero and Sporo's Relationship" provides a comprehensive overview of their historical love story and serves as a valuable resource for historians and wedding enthusiasts alike. From detailed accounts of their relationship to practical advice on planning an unforgettable historical-themed wedding, this subchapter offers a wealth of information to inspire and captivate readers.

Historical Context: Rome during the reign of Nero

In this subchapter, we explore the historical context of Rome during the reign of Nero, providing a backdrop for the events that unfold in "The Wedding Between Nero and Sporo." As historians, it is important to understand the societal, political, and cultural aspects of this period to fully appreciate the significance of this love story.

Nero, the fifth Roman Emperor, ascended to the throne in 54 AD at the tender age of 16. His reign marked a turning point in Roman history, characterized by political intrigue, cultural innovation, and scandalous affairs. Rome, at this time, was a city of contrasts, with vast wealth and opulence alongside deep poverty and social unrest.

Nero's rule began with great promise, as he initially embraced a policy of appeasement towards the Senate and the people of Rome. However, as time went on, his reign was marred by a series of controversies and excesses that would eventually lead to his downfall. Nero's love affair with Sporo, a young freedman and charioteer, was just one of the scandalous relationships that rocked the Roman elite.

"The Wedding Between Nero and Sporo" explores the forbidden love between the Emperor and his beloved, challenging the norms of the time. It delves into the complexities of their relationship, shedding light on the LGBTQ+ community in ancient Rome and their struggles for acceptance.

For historians interested in wedding planning for historical themed weddings, this subchapter provides valuable insights into Roman wedding traditions and rituals. From the betrothal ceremony to the exchange of vows, readers will gain a deeper understanding of how love was celebrated during this period. Additionally, it offers inspiration for those interested in organizing unique wedding venues that transport guests back to the grandeur of ancient Rome.

With a focus on historical wedding attire and fashion, this subchapter also explores the elaborate costumes and accessories worn by both the bride and groom during Roman weddings. It highlights the importance of aesthetics and symbolism in ancient Roman culture, providing invaluable information for historians and enthusiasts alike.

Furthermore, for those seeking inspiration for historical wedding photography and videography, this subchapter offers a glimpse into the visual aesthetics of ancient Rome. It discusses the unique challenges and opportunities that arise when capturing the essence of a historical love story, providing practical advice for photographers and videographers.

In conclusion, the historical context of Rome during the reign of Nero is a crucial element in understanding "The Wedding Between Nero and Sporo." It provides historians, wedding planners, and enthusiasts with a deeper appreciation for the cultural, social, and political landscape of ancient Rome, offering insights into Roman wedding traditions, fashion, and the LGBTQ+ community.

The Forbidden Love: Nero and Sporo's Secret Relationship

"The Forbidden Love: Nero and Sporo's Secret Relationship"

In the annals of history, there are tales of love that transcend time, defying societal norms and challenging the boundaries of conventionality. One such story is the forbidden love affair between Emperor Nero and his beloved Sporo. This subchapter explores the clandestine relationship between these two historical figures, shedding light on their profound bond and the challenges they faced as they navigated their love in the midst of ancient Rome.

Nero, known for his controversial reign, was an emperor feared and revered in equal measure. However, behind the facade of power, lay a deeply hidden secret – his love for Sporo, a young slave of exquisite beauty. In an era where same-sex relationships were frowned upon, Nero and Sporo's love was a forbidden treasure, hidden away from prying eyes.

Theirs was a love that defied the constraints of societal expectations. Nero, consumed by his passion for Sporo, disregarded the consequences that their love may bring. They reveled in stolen moments, sharing tender embraces and whispered promises in the shadows of the Roman empire.

This subchapter delves into the challenges faced by Nero and Sporo as they sought to protect their love. It explores the ways in which they managed to keep their relationship a secret, despite the ever-watchful eyes of the Roman court. It also sheds light on the strategies employed by the couple to navigate the treacherous waters of ancient Rome, where their love could have dire consequences.

For historians, this story of forbidden love offers a rare glimpse into the personal lives of two historical figures who defied convention. It provides an opportunity to explore the complexities of love in a society where it was deemed unacceptable. The tale of Nero and Sporo serves as a reminder that love knows no boundaries, and that even in the most oppressive of circumstances, the human spirit can prevail.

This subchapter will appeal not only to historians, but also to those interested in wedding planning for historical-themed weddings. It offers inspiration for Roman Empire-inspired wedding themes, LGBTQ+ historical weddings, and unique wedding venues for historical enthusiasts. It also provides insights into ancient Roman wedding traditions and rituals, historical wedding attire and fashion, as well as historical wedding photography and videography. Moreover, it serves as a guide for incorporating historical elements into wedding favors, decorations, and reception entertainment, giving a unique historical twist to any wedding celebration.

In conclusion, "The Forbidden Love: Nero and Sporo's Secret Relationship" is a captivating subchapter that unravels a timeless love story in the annals of history. It appeals to historians and various niches within the wedding industry, offering a rich tapestry of inspiration and insights into the extraordinary love shared between Nero and Sporo.

Chapter 2: Wedding Planning for Historical Themed Weddings

Choosing a Historical Theme for Your Wedding

When it comes to planning your wedding, there are countless themes to choose from. However, if you are a history enthusiast, why not consider a historical theme for your special day? From ancient civilizations to more recent eras, incorporating history into your wedding can add a unique and romantic touch. In this subchapter, we will explore various historical themes that you can incorporate into your wedding, ensuring a truly memorable and one-of-a-kind celebration.

One popular historical theme for weddings is based on the love story between Nero and Sporo. This infamous Roman emperor and his beloved slave provide a captivating backdrop for a wedding ceremony. By drawing inspiration from their relationship, you can create a wedding that is both historically significant and deeply romantic.

For those interested in ancient Roman wedding traditions and rituals, incorporating these customs into your own ceremony can bring a touch of authenticity to your special day. From the exchange of vows to the wearing of wreaths, these ancient traditions can add a sense of timelessness to your wedding.

When it comes to wedding attire and fashion, historical themes offer a wealth of inspiration. Whether you choose to don a Roman toga or a Renaissance-inspired gown, incorporating historical elements into your attire can make you feel like a true historical figure on your big day.

To capture the essence of your historical wedding, consider hiring a photographer and videographer who specialize in historical reenactments. These professionals can help you create stunning visual memories that will transport you and your guests back in time.

When it comes to wedding favors and decorations, there are endless possibilities for historical enthusiasts. From Roman-inspired trinkets to medieval-style centerpieces, incorporating historical elements into your decor can create a truly immersive experience for your guests.

Finally, for entertainment at your wedding reception, consider hiring performers who specialize in historical reenactments. Whether it's a troupe of Roman gladiators or a medieval minstrel, these entertainers can provide a unique and memorable experience for you and your guests.

In conclusion, choosing a historical theme for your wedding can add a truly unique and romantic touch to your special day. Whether you are a fan of ancient civilizations, the Roman empire, or more recent eras, there are countless ways to incorporate history into your wedding. From the venue to the attire, the photography to the favors, there are endless possibilities for creating a wedding that captures the magic of the past. So, embrace your love of history and create a wedding that will be remembered for years to come.

Researching Historical Wedding Traditions and Rituals

When planning a wedding with a historical theme, it is essential to research and understand the historical wedding traditions and rituals that will be incorporated into the event. This subchapter aims to guide historians, enthusiasts of the Nero and Sporo love story, and those interested in historical-themed weddings to delve into the rich tapestry of ancient Roman wedding customs.

Ancient Rome offers a treasure trove of wedding traditions and rituals that can be adapted and modernized for contemporary celebrations. From the pre-wedding rituals to the ceremony itself, every step was filled with symbolism and significance. Historians can explore the significance of the Roman engagement period, the roles of family and community, and the elaborate preparations leading up to the wedding day.

For those fascinated by LGBTQ+ historical weddings, the story of Nero and Sporo is particularly relevant. Their wedding, considered groundbreaking even in ancient times, can serve as an inspiration for couples seeking to honor historical LGBTQ+ relationships in their own ceremonies. Understanding the historical context of their union and the challenges they faced can add depth and meaning to the wedding planning process.

One aspect that historians and wedding planners can explore is the attire and fashion of ancient Roman weddings. Researching the fashion trends of the time, the fabrics used, and the significance of certain accessories can help in recreating historically accurate wedding attire. This knowledge can also guide couples in finding or designing wedding outfits that evoke the spirit of the ancient Roman era.

Additionally, historians and enthusiasts can delve into the art of historical wedding photography and videography. Understanding the aesthetics and techniques prevalent in ancient times can help capture the essence of the wedding in a way that is reminiscent of historical imagery.

For those interested in unique wedding venues, this subchapter can provide guidance on finding locations that cater to historical enthusiasts. From ancient Roman ruins to grand historical estates, there are numerous venues that can transport guests back in time and create an immersive experience.

Lastly, for those seeking entertainment with a historical twist during the wedding reception, this subchapter can explore various options. Ideas such as historical reenactments, performances by period musicians, or even interactive activities can make the celebration truly unforgettable.

In conclusion, researching historical wedding traditions and rituals is crucial for historians, wedding planners, and enthusiasts alike. Whether it is delving into the love story of Nero and Sporo, exploring ancient Roman customs, or finding inspiration for unique wedding elements, this subchapter serves as a comprehensive guide for creating an extraordinary historical-themed wedding experience.

Incorporating Historical Elements into Wedding Invitations and Stationery

When it comes to planning a wedding, every detail counts. For historians and enthusiasts of historical-themed weddings, incorporating historical elements into wedding invitations and stationery can add an extra layer of authenticity and charm to your special day. In this subchapter, we will explore various ways to infuse history into your wedding invitations, from ancient Roman-inspired designs to LGBTQ+ historical weddings.

One of the most popular historical themes for weddings is the Roman Empire. Drawing inspiration from this ancient civilization, your wedding invitations can feature Roman motifs such as laurel wreaths, togas, or intricate mosaic patterns. By using fonts reminiscent of ancient Roman calligraphy, you can transport your guests back in time, setting the tone for an unforgettable wedding experience.

For LGBTQ+ couples looking to celebrate their love while honoring historical figures and events, incorporating elements from LGBTQ+ historical weddings is a wonderful way to pay homage to the struggle and triumphs of the past. Consider including symbols like the pink triangle or the rainbow flag in your wedding invitations, symbolizing unity and resilience.

In addition to design, historical wedding invitations can also incorporate ancient Roman wedding traditions and rituals. Including a brief explanation of these customs, such as the exchanging of rings, crowning the couple with laurel wreaths, or the breaking of a cake over the bride's head, will not only educate your guests but also immerse them in the historical significance of your special day.

To further enhance the historical ambiance, consider using vintage-inspired materials for your wedding invitations and stationery. Parchment-like paper, wax seals, or even handwritten calligraphy can transport your guests to a bygone era. Adding historically accurate maps or illustrations of unique wedding venues for historical enthusiasts can also provide a glimpse into the location's historical significance.

Lastly, don't forget to capture your historical-themed wedding in all its glory. Hire a professional photographer and videographer who specialize in historical weddings to ensure your memories are preserved in a way that reflects the grandeur and uniqueness of your special day.

Remember, your wedding invitations and stationery are the first glimpse your guests will have into your historical-themed wedding. By incorporating historical elements into these crucial elements, you can set the stage for an unforgettable celebration that honors the past while embracing the present.

Selecting Historical-inspired Wedding Attire

One of the most exciting aspects of planning a historical-themed wedding is choosing the perfect attire that will transport you and your guests back in time. The attire you select not only reflects the historical era you have chosen but also adds a touch of authenticity to your special day. Whether you are recreating the grandeur of the Roman Empire or celebrating a LGBTQ+ love story in the past, here are some tips to help you select the perfect historical-inspired wedding attire.

Research is key when it comes to selecting historical-inspired wedding attire. Start by immersing yourself in the era you wish to recreate. Explore paintings, photographs, and historical documents that showcase the fashion of the time. This research will give you a better understanding of the silhouettes, fabrics, and embellishments that were popular during that era.

Once you have a clear vision of the era, it's time to start shopping for your wedding attire. Look for designers or boutiques that specialize in historical fashion. They will have the expertise to create or source authentic-looking garments that are tailored to your specific needs. Alternatively, you can also consider renting or purchasing vintage garments from reputable sellers.

When selecting historical-inspired wedding attire, pay attention to the details. Choose fabrics that were commonly used during the era, such as silk, brocade, or lace. Incorporate historical elements like corsets, bustles, or crinolines to achieve the desired silhouette. Don't forget to accessorize with historically accurate jewelry, headpieces, and footwear to complete your look.

For LGBTQ+ historical weddings, it is essential to find attire that reflects the time period while also celebrating your unique love story. Look for historical examples of same-sex unions or explore gender-bending fashion from the past for inspiration. Embrace your individuality and don't be afraid to make a statement with your attire.

Once you have chosen your historical-inspired wedding attire, consider incorporating it into other aspects of your wedding. Coordinate the attire of your wedding party to complement your own, creating a cohesive and visually stunning ensemble. Work with your photographer and videographer to capture the essence of the era through carefully planned shots and poses.

In conclusion, selecting historical-inspired wedding attire is an exciting and crucial part of planning a historical-themed wedding. By thoroughly researching the era, working with experienced designers or vintage sellers, paying attention to authentic details, and celebrating your unique love story, you can create an unforgettable wedding that transports you and your guests back in time. Let the past inspire your present and make your wedding an unforgettable historical experience.

Planning a Historical-inspired Wedding Menu

When it comes to planning a historical-inspired wedding, a crucial aspect to consider is the menu. The food and drink served at your wedding can transport your guests back in time, immersing them in the historical ambiance of your special day. In this subchapter, we will explore various ideas and tips for creating a memorable and authentic historical wedding menu.

Drawing inspiration from the wedding between Nero and Sporo, a historical love story, we can delve into the Roman Empire for a truly unique wedding experience. The Roman cuisine was known for its rich flavors and diverse ingredients, making it an excellent choice for a historical-themed wedding.

Start your menu with an array of appetizers reminiscent of ancient Rome. Consider serving stuffed dates, marinated olives, and cheese platters featuring a selection of artisanal cheeses. These small bites will tantalize your guests' taste buds and set the stage for the main course.

For the main course, options such as roasted meats, grilled fish, and vegetable stews will pay homage to the traditional Roman feasts. Consider incorporating dishes like roasted lamb with herbs, honey-glazed quail, or a hearty vegetable minestrone. Accompany these dishes with a selection of Roman-inspired sides such as garum-infused roasted vegetables or spelt salad.

To satisfy your guests' sweet tooth, offer a variety of desserts that reflect the Roman era. Options can include honey cakes, almond pastries, and fruit tarts. Don't forget to include Roman-inspired beverages such as mulsum, a sweetened wine mixed with honey and spices, or posca, a refreshing vinegar-based drink.

Creating a historical-inspired wedding menu goes beyond the food. Consider incorporating historical elements into your table settings and decorations. Use Roman-inspired tableware, such as terracotta plates or goblets, and adorn the tables with olive branches and laurel wreaths.

To further enhance the historical ambiance, consider hiring a historical reenactment group to provide entertainment during the reception. They can perform traditional Roman dances or showcase gladiator fights, adding an unforgettable touch to your special day.

Capture the essence of your historical-themed wedding by hiring a skilled photographer and videographer that specialize in historical weddings. They will understand the significance of capturing the intricate details and moments that make your event unique.

Lastly, send your guests home with historical wedding favors that reflect the Roman era. Consider gifting them small bottles of olive oil, personalized Roman coins, or even miniature replicas of Roman artifacts.

Planning a historical-inspired wedding menu is an opportunity to transport your guests back in time and create an unforgettable experience. By incorporating authentic Roman dishes, historical elements, and unique entertainment, your wedding will be a celebration that leaves a lasting impression on both you and your guests.

Chapter 3: Historical Reenactment Weddings

The Rise of Historical Reenactment Weddings

Throughout history, weddings have always been a celebration of love, commitment, and the merging of two families. But in recent years, a new trend has emerged that takes the concept of a traditional wedding to a whole new level. Welcome to the world of historical reenactment weddings, where couples and their guests step back in time to say their vows in the style of an era long gone.

One of the most fascinating historical love stories that has captured the imaginations of historians and romantics alike is that of Nero and Sporo. This epic tale of forbidden love between the Roman Emperor Nero and his male slave Sporo has become the inspiration for many historical-themed weddings. The book "The Wedding Between Nero and Sporo: A Historical Love Story" delves into their extraordinary relationship, providing a rich source of inspiration for couples looking to plan their own unique wedding.

For historians and enthusiasts of the Roman Empire, a wedding inspired by Nero and Sporo allows them to immerse themselves in the opulence and grandeur of ancient Rome. From the decorations and favors to the attire and rituals, every aspect of the wedding can transport guests back in time. Imagine walking down the aisle in a stunning Roman-inspired gown or exchanging vows in a replica of the Colosseum. The possibilities are endless.

These historical reenactment weddings are not limited to heterosexual couples either. LGBTQ+ couples can also find inspiration in the stories of historical same-sex relationships and celebrate their love in a way that pays homage to their shared history.

In addition to the historical theme, these weddings offer unique venues that cater to the interests of history buffs. From ancient ruins to castles and museums, couples can choose a location that adds an extra layer of authenticity to their special day.

Photography and videography play a crucial role in capturing the essence of a historical reenactment wedding. With skilled professionals who specialize in historical weddings, couples can have their love story immortalized in a way that reflects the aesthetics of the chosen era.

To complete the experience, wedding reception entertainment can take on a historical twist. From period music and dance performances to interactive games and storytelling, guests will be transported back in time, creating memories that will last a lifetime.

Whether you're a historian, a lover of all things historical, or simply someone who wants to create a wedding that stands out from the crowd, the rise of historical reenactment weddings offers a unique opportunity to celebrate love while honoring the past. So, step back in time and let history be the backdrop for your own unforgettable love story.

Finding the Perfect Historical Reenactment Venue

When it comes to planning a historical themed wedding, one of the most crucial decisions is choosing the perfect venue. The right location can transport you and your guests back in time, creating an immersive experience that will make your special day truly unforgettable. Whether you are a historian, a lover of historical reenactments, or simply seeking a unique wedding venue, here are some tips to help you find the perfect historical reenactment venue for your wedding.

First and foremost, consider the theme of your wedding. If you are inspired by the love story between Emperor Nero and his beloved Sporo, why not search for a venue that resembles ancient Rome? Look for venues that feature architectural elements reminiscent of the Roman

Empire, such as columns, arches, and grand courtyards. These details will enhance the authenticity of your wedding and transport you and your guests back to the time of Nero and Sporo.

For LGBTQ+ couples who wish to celebrate their love with a historical twist, consider venues that are not only historically significant but also inclusive. Look for locations that have hosted LGBTQ+ historical events or have a strong connection to LGBTQ+ history. This will add a deeper layer of meaning to your wedding and allow you to celebrate your love in a place that has a rich historical and cultural significance for the LGBTQ+ community.

Additionally, think about the practical aspects of your wedding. Consider the size of the venue and whether it can accommodate your guest list comfortably. Look for venues that offer amenities such as dressing rooms, parking, and catering facilities. It's also important to consider the accessibility of the venue for your guests, especially if you have elderly or disabled attendees.

Finally, don't forget about the smaller details that will make your wedding truly authentic. Look for venues that allow you to incorporate ancient Roman wedding traditions and rituals into your ceremony. Consider hiring historical wedding reenactors to add a touch of authenticity to your celebration. Think about providing historical wedding favors and decorations that reflect the time period and theme of your wedding. Lastly, don't forget to hire a professional photographer and videographer who specialize in capturing historical weddings, as their expertise will ensure that your special day is documented in a way that truly reflects the essence of the time.

In conclusion, finding the perfect historical reenactment venue for your wedding requires careful consideration of the theme, practical aspects, and smaller details that will make your celebration truly authentic. By taking the time to research and explore different venues, you can create a wedding experience that transports you and your guests back in time, allowing you to celebrate your love in a truly unique and memorable way.

Historical Reenactment Wedding Roles and Etiquette

In the enchanting world of historical reenactment weddings, every detail holds significance, from the meticulous recreation of ancient rituals to the elegant attire that transports guests back in time. This subchapter delves into the captivating realm of historical wedding roles and etiquette, providing a comprehensive guide for historians and enthusiasts alike.

One of the key aspects of historical reenactment weddings is the emphasis on authenticity. To truly immerse oneself in the experience, it is essential to meticulously recreate the roles and etiquette of the era being portrayed. In the case of the wedding between Nero and Sporo, understanding the dynamics of the Roman Empire is crucial.

During Roman times, weddings were seen as a significant event not only for the couple but also for the entire community. The subchapter explores the roles of key individuals, such as the bride and groom, the parents, and the bridal party. It examines the specific responsibilities and expectations placed upon each role, shedding light on the social and cultural nuances of Roman society.

Etiquette also played a vital role in ancient Roman weddings. From the proper way to address guests to the appropriate behavior during the ceremony, understanding the intricacies of Roman etiquette adds an authentic touch to historical reenactment weddings. The subchapter provides insights into the do's and don'ts of Roman wedding etiquette, offering valuable guidance for those planning a Roman Empire-inspired wedding.

Beyond the historical context, the subchapter also explores the intersection between historical reenactment weddings and contemporary issues, such as LGBTQ+ historical weddings. It highlights the challenges faced by same-sex couples in historical eras and offers creative solutions to incorporate LGBTQ+ narratives into reenactment weddings.

Furthermore, the subchapter delves into the practical aspects of planning a historical reenactment wedding. It provides invaluable advice on finding unique wedding venues that cater to historical enthusiasts, as well as suggestions for incorporating ancient Roman wedding traditions and rituals into the ceremony. From wedding attire and fashion to photography, videography, favors, decorations, and reception entertainment, every element is explored through a historical lens.

Whether you are a historian seeking to recreate the past or an enthusiast planning a unique wedding experience, this subchapter serves as a comprehensive guide to historical reenactment wedding roles and etiquette. Immerse yourself in the fascinating world of ancient Rome and create a wedding that will be remembered for centuries to come.

Hiring Historical Reenactors for Your Wedding

For those who are passionate about history and want to create a wedding that truly stands out, hiring historical reenactors can add a unique and immersive touch to your special day. Whether you are a historian, a fan of the Roman Empire, or simply love the idea of a historical-themed wedding, incorporating reenactors can transport you and your guests back in time and create an unforgettable experience.

One popular historical love story that has captured the imagination of many is the romance between Nero and Sporo. Their controversial relationship, set against the backdrop of the Roman Empire, is a tale of love, power, and defiance. By hiring historical reenactors to portray Nero and Sporo, you can bring their story to life and make your wedding a true celebration of history.

Planning a historical-themed wedding can be a daunting task, but with the right resources and guidance, it can also be an incredibly rewarding experience. From finding unique wedding venues that capture the essence of the Roman Empire to incorporating ancient Roman wedding traditions and rituals, there are countless ways to infuse history into your special day.

When it comes to attire and fashion, historical weddings offer a plethora of options. From elegant Roman togas to intricate Byzantine gowns, the choices are endless. By working with a talented designer, you can create custom-made outfits that will transport you and your partner to a different era.

Capturing the essence of your historical wedding through photography and videography is also crucial. Hiring professionals who specialize in historical weddings can ensure that every moment is beautifully documented, allowing you to relive the magic for years to come.

To add an extra touch of authenticity, consider incorporating historical wedding favors and decorations. From Roman coins to miniature replicas of ancient artifacts, these unique and thoughtful gifts will serve as a reminder of your unforgettable day.

Finally, no wedding is complete without entertainment. Hiring historical reenactors to perform during your reception can be a fantastic way to keep your guests entertained while staying true to the theme. From gladiator fights to traditional Roman dances, the possibilities are endless.

In conclusion, hiring historical reenactors for your wedding can elevate your special day to a whole new level. With careful planning and attention to detail, you can create a truly immersive and unforgettable experience that will leave a lasting impression on you and your guests. Whether you are a historian, an enthusiast of the Roman Empire, or simply want a unique and memorable wedding, incorporating historical elements into your celebration is sure to create an event that will be talked about for years to come.

Chapter 4: Roman Empire-inspired Wedding Themes

The Allure of the Roman Empire for Wedding Themes

In the realm of wedding planning, there is a growing fascination with historical themes, offering couples the opportunity to transport their guests to a bygone era. One such era that has captivated the imagination of many is the Roman Empire. Its opulence, grandeur, and rich cultural heritage make it an ideal choice for couples seeking a unique and memorable wedding celebration.

The Wedding Between Nero and Sporo: A Historical Love Story, delves into the captivating tale of Emperor Nero and his beloved Sporo, offering historians and enthusiasts a glimpse into their extraordinary love affair. This subchapter explores the allure of the Roman Empire for wedding themes, exploring various aspects that make it an irresistible choice for couples and historians alike.

One of the key draws of a Roman Empire-inspired wedding theme is the opportunity to recreate the splendor of the ancient empire. From the majestic architecture to the sumptuous fashion, couples can immerse themselves and their guests in the grandeur of a bygone era. Imagine exchanging vows in a stunning outdoor venue reminiscent of the Colosseum, with guests adorned in elegant Roman attire, creating a truly unforgettable experience.

For LGBTQ+ couples, an ancient Roman theme holds a particular appeal. The love story of Nero and Sporo, two men defying societal norms, serves as a powerful symbol of love overcoming adversity. By incorporating LGBTQ+ historical weddings into the subchapter, we aim to shed light on the diverse representation of love throughout history.

When planning a historically themed wedding, choosing the right venue is crucial. Historical enthusiasts will find inspiration in unique wedding venues like ancient ruins or historical landmarks, transporting them back in time and creating an atmosphere of authenticity.

To fully immerse guests in the Roman Empire experience, incorporating ancient traditions and rituals is essential. The subchapter will delve into ancient Roman wedding customs, such as the exchange of rings, the significance of the veil, and the importance of the wedding banquet.

Furthermore, this chapter will explore historical wedding attire and fashion, showcasing the opulent Roman garments, hairstyles, and accessories that can elevate any wedding celebration. The subchapter will also touch on the importance of historical wedding photography and videography, capturing the essence of the Roman Empire and preserving the memories for years to come.

No wedding is complete without thoughtful details, and a Roman Empire-inspired theme provides a wealth of options for historical wedding favors and decorations. From Roman-inspired centerpieces to personalized Roman coins, these details will transport guests into the realm of ancient Rome.

Lastly, a wedding reception with a historical twist is not complete without entertainment that reflects the era. The subchapter will explore various options, from gladiator reenactments to ancient Roman dance performances, ensuring that guests are thoroughly entertained throughout the celebration.

In summary, the allure of the Roman Empire for wedding themes is undeniable. This subchapter aims to provide historians and enthusiasts with a comprehensive guide to planning a wedding inspired by the grandeur and romance of ancient Rome. From historical reenactments to unique venues, this chapter will serve as a valuable resource for those seeking to create a truly unforgettable wedding experience.

Incorporating Roman-inspired Decorations and Favors

When planning a historical-themed wedding, incorporating Roman-inspired decorations and favors can transport you and your guests back in time to the grandeur of the Roman Empire. Whether you're a history enthusiast, a lover of ancient traditions, or an LGBTQ+ couple seeking a unique wedding experience, this subchapter explores how to infuse your special day with the essence of ancient Rome.

To create an authentic Roman atmosphere, start with the decorations. Adorn your venue with classical columns, reminiscent of those found in Roman architecture. Draping sheer fabrics in rich colors, such as deep reds and purples, will evoke the luxurious ambiance of a Roman banquet hall. Consider incorporating laurel wreaths, symbolic of victory and honor, into your floral arrangements and table centerpieces. Roman-style pottery and statues can also be used as decorative accents, adding an air of authenticity to your event.

When it comes to favors, think about items that reflect the spirit of ancient Rome. Miniature replicas of Roman coins or gladiator helmets can make for unique and memorable gifts. Consider providing guests with personalized wax seals and scrolls, reminiscent of the Roman practice of sealing important documents. These can be used to create personalized thank-you notes or to commemorate the occasion.

For those looking to provide entertainment with a historical twist, consider hiring historical reenactors to engage your guests. They can perform gladiator fights, showcase traditional Roman dances, or even give interactive historical presentations. This will not only captivate your guests but also give them a chance to immerse themselves in the rich history of the Roman Empire.

To capture the essence of a Roman wedding, pay special attention to your attire. Roman-inspired togas or tunics can be worn by the wedding party, while the couple can opt for elegant Roman-style gowns and accessories. Incorporating traditional Roman hairstyles and jewelry will add an extra touch of authenticity.

Finally, don't forget to hire a photographer and videographer who specialize in historical weddings. They will have the expertise to capture the unique details and atmosphere of your Roman-inspired celebration, ensuring that the memories of your special day are preserved for years to come.

Overall, incorporating Roman-inspired decorations and favors into your wedding will transport you and your guests to a bygone era. By embracing the rich history of the Roman Empire, you can create a truly unforgettable experience that pays homage to the ancient traditions and celebrates your love in a unique and meaningful way.

Roman-inspired Wedding Attire and Fashion

The wedding between Emperor Nero and his beloved Sporo was a significant event in the history of the Roman Empire, and as historians, it is important for us to delve into the intricate details of this grand celebration. One aspect that captivated the attendees and continues to fascinate us today is the exquisite Roman-inspired wedding attire and fashion.

In ancient Rome, weddings were occasions to display wealth, status, and fashion sense. The bride and groom, as well as their guests, adorned themselves in luxurious fabrics, intricate designs, and opulent accessories. For a Roman-inspired wedding, couples can draw inspiration from this grandeur to create a memorable and historically accurate experience.

The bride can channel the elegance and grace of Roman women by wearing a flowing, floor-length white tunic known as a stola. This garment, adorned with delicate embroidery and intricate patterns, symbolized purity and marital bliss. The stola could be paired with a colorful palla, a draped shawl that added a touch of sophistication.

For the groom, a toga or a tunic with a purple or red color palette would be a fitting choice. These colors were associated with royalty and power in ancient Rome. The groom could also wear a laurel wreath as a crown, symbolizing victory and honor.

Guests attending a Roman-inspired wedding can embrace the fashion of the time by wearing tunics, stolas, or even togas made from lightweight fabrics. They can accessorize with sandals, jewelry, and headpieces that reflect the opulence of the Roman Empire.

To capture the essence of this historical love story, couples can opt for photographers and videographers who specialize in historical weddings. These professionals have a keen eye for detail and can create stunning visuals that transport viewers back to ancient Rome.

When it comes to wedding favors and decorations, couples can incorporate Roman-inspired elements such as laurel wreaths, Roman coins, or miniature replicas of famous Roman landmarks. These unique gifts will serve as cherished reminders of the celebration for years to come.

For the reception, couples can surprise their guests with entertainment that has a historical twist. They can hire reenactors who can perform traditional Roman dances or engage guests in interactive games that were popular during that era.

In conclusion, Roman-inspired wedding attire and fashion offer a unique opportunity for couples to immerse themselves in the rich history and grandeur of the Roman Empire. By carefully selecting historically accurate garments and accessories, couples can create a wedding that will be remembered by historians and enthusiasts alike for its authenticity and elegance.

Roman-inspired Wedding Menu and Cuisine

When it comes to planning a historical-themed wedding, one of the most important aspects to consider is the menu and cuisine. For those who are fascinated by the Roman Empire and its rich culinary traditions, a Roman-inspired wedding menu will transport guests back in time and create a truly memorable experience.

The Roman cuisine was known for its extravagant feasts and diverse flavors. Incorporating these elements into your wedding menu will not only satisfy your guests' taste buds but also provide a unique and immersive dining experience.

Start off the wedding reception with an assortment of appetizers inspired by ancient Rome. Offer a selection of cheeses, olives, and bread accompanied by figs, grapes, and honey. These simple yet flavorful bites were staples in ancient Roman cuisine and will set the tone for the rest of the meal.

For the main course, consider serving a succulent roasted meat dish, such as pork or lamb, seasoned with herbs and spices that were commonly used in ancient Rome. Accompany it with a variety of seasonal vegetables and grains like barley or farro. This will give your guests a taste of the Roman Empire's agricultural practices and dietary habits.

To add a touch of extravagance, consider serving a Roman-style seafood dish, such as a seafood stew or grilled fish. The Romans were known for their love of seafood, and incorporating this element into your menu will add a touch of authenticity and luxury to the dining experience.

No Roman-inspired wedding menu would be complete without a selection of decadent desserts. Offer sweet treats like honey cakes, spiced nuts, and fresh fruits drizzled with honey. These desserts were enjoyed by Romans and will provide a sweet ending to the meal.

To enhance the overall experience, consider hiring a professional chef who specializes in ancient Roman cuisine or collaborating with a catering company that can recreate these dishes authentically.

In conclusion, a Roman-inspired wedding menu will transport your guests back in time and create a truly memorable experience. By incorporating the flavors and culinary traditions of ancient Rome into your wedding feast, you will not only satisfy your guests' taste buds but also provide a unique and immersive dining experience that will be talked about for years to come.

Chapter 5: LGBTQ+ Historical Weddings

The Challenges Faced by LGBTQ+ Couples in History

Throughout history, LGBTQ+ couples have faced numerous challenges in their pursuit of love and acceptance. In this subchapter, we will explore the struggles faced by LGBTQ+ couples in different historical periods, shedding light on the discrimination and oppression they endured.

In ancient Rome, where our love story between Nero and Sporo unfolds, LGBTQ+ relationships faced both societal and legal barriers. Homosexuality was not only frowned upon but was also considered a crime. Despite this, Nero and Sporo's love managed to flourish, albeit in secrecy. Their story serves as a reminder of the resilience and strength exhibited by LGBTQ+ couples in the face of adversity.

Moving forward in history, LGBTQ+ couples faced further challenges during the Victorian era. The strict moral codes and conservative values of the time led to the suppression of same-sex relationships. LGBTQ+ individuals were forced to hide their true identities, leading to a life of secrecy and fear. The struggles faced during this period highlight the importance of understanding and acknowledging the historical struggles of the LGBTQ+ community.

In the 20th century, LGBTQ+ couples faced discrimination in the form of legal and social barriers. Same-sex relationships were deemed illegal in many countries, making it difficult for LGBTQ+ couples to openly express their love. It wasn't until the Stonewall riots in 1969 that the LGBTQ+ rights movement gained momentum, leading to significant changes in legislation and societal attitudes.

Despite these challenges, LGBTQ+ couples have managed to find love and celebrate their unions throughout history. Today, we can draw inspiration from their stories and strive for a more inclusive society. The Wedding Between Nero and Sporo serves as a reminder that love knows no boundaries, and that LGBTQ+ couples have always existed and thrived, even in the face of adversity.

For historians and enthusiasts of historical weddings, this subchapter sheds light on the struggles faced by LGBTQ+ couples throughout history. It invites a deeper understanding of the challenges they encountered and the resilience they displayed. By recognizing their stories, we can ensure that LGBTQ+ history is not forgotten, and that the struggles faced by LGBTQ+ couples in the past are acknowledged and learned from.

This subchapter will serve as a valuable resource for historians, wedding planners, and individuals interested in LGBTQ+ history, providing insights into the challenges faced by LGBTQ+ couples and the progress made towards a more inclusive society. It will contribute to the broader conversation surrounding LGBTQ+ rights and representation in historical narratives, ensuring that their stories are not erased but celebrated.

Celebrating LGBTQ+ Love through Historical Themes

In today's modern society, love knows no boundaries, and the LGBTQ+ community has fought tirelessly for their rights and recognition. However, it is essential to acknowledge that same-sex love is not a recent phenomenon. Throughout history, there have been countless examples of LGBTQ+ individuals who defied societal norms and found love in the most extraordinary circumstances. "The Wedding Between Nero and Sporo: A Historical Love Story" explores one such remarkable tale.

This subchapter delves into the celebration of LGBTQ+ love through historical themes, catering to the interests of historians and various niches such as wedding planning for historical themed weddings, historical reenactment weddings, Roman empire-inspired wedding themes, and LGBTQ+ historical weddings.

Historians and enthusiasts of the book "The Wedding Between Nero and Sporo" will find inspiration in exploring unique wedding venues for historical enthusiasts. From ancient ruins and grand castles to historic landmarks, there are endless possibilities to create an authentic and memorable setting for a wedding steeped in history.

Additionally, this chapter uncovers ancient Roman wedding traditions and rituals, providing valuable insights into the customs of that era. Readers will learn about the significance of the matrimonial ceremony and the symbolism behind various rituals, helping them incorporate these elements into their own LGBTQ+ historical weddings.

For those interested in historical wedding attire and fashion, this subchapter explores the fascinating world of ancient Roman clothing and accessories. From flowing togas to intricate headpieces, there are countless possibilities to design unique and historically accurate wedding attire for LGBTQ+ couples wanting to celebrate their love in a historically inspired way.

Furthermore, this subchapter delves into the art of historical wedding photography and videography. With the help of professional photographers and videographers experienced in capturing historical reenactments, LGBTQ+ couples can immortalize their special day in a manner that truly reflects their love and the historical context they wish to honor.

To enhance the overall ambiance of a historical-themed wedding, readers will also find inspiration for historical wedding favors and decorations.

From Roman-inspired trinkets to ancient-inspired centerpieces, these elements will transport guests to a bygone era, creating an unforgettable experience.

Lastly, for those seeking unique wedding reception entertainment with a historical twist, this subchapter suggests various options. From historically accurate performances to interactive reenactments, these entertainment choices will ensure that guests are fully immersed in the historical theme of the wedding.

In conclusion, "Celebrating LGBTQ+ Love through Historical Themes" is a subchapter that aims to inspire historians and enthusiasts of "The Wedding Between Nero and Sporo" to explore and celebrate LGBTQ+ love in a historically accurate and meaningful way. From ancient Roman wedding traditions to unique wedding venues and historical reenactments, this subchapter offers a wealth of information and ideas to make every LGBTQ+ historical wedding a truly memorable and authentic experience.

LGBTQ+ Wedding Traditions and Rituals through History

Throughout history, LGBTQ+ individuals have faced numerous challenges in expressing their love and commitment to one another openly. However, even in times when same-sex relationships were not widely accepted, love still found a way to flourish. In this subchapter, we will explore the fascinating history of LGBTQ+ wedding traditions and rituals, shedding light on the resilience and strength of these couples.

One of the most remarkable stories that exemplify LGBTQ+ love is that of Emperor Nero and his lover Sporo in ancient Rome. Despite the conservative societal norms, Nero declared a public wedding ceremony between the two, creating a precedent for same-sex unions. This act challenged traditional Roman views on marriage and demonstrated the existence of same-sex relationships in ancient times.

In understanding LGBTQ+ wedding traditions throughout history, it is crucial to recognize the influence of cultural and religious beliefs. In some Native American tribes, for instance, Two-Spirit individuals held significant roles during wedding ceremonies, symbolizing the balance of masculine and feminine energies. These sacred unions were celebrated and respected within their communities.

For historians interested in planning historical-themed weddings, incorporating LGBTQ+ traditions can add depth and authenticity to the event. Roman empire-inspired wedding themes, for example, could include a reenactment of Nero and Sporo's symbolic union, reflecting their love and courage.

When it comes to attire and fashion, historical LGBTQ+ weddings were often marked by unconventional choices that challenged gender norms. Incorporating these elements into modern wedding fashion can celebrate the diversity and individuality of LGBTQ+ couples.

Capturing the essence of a historical LGBTQ+ wedding is essential, and historical wedding photography and videography can transport couples and viewers back in time. By using techniques inspired by the past, photographers and videographers can create stunning visuals that reflect the emotions and spirit of the occasion.

To add an extra touch of historical charm to LGBTQ+ weddings, couples can consider unique venues that resonate with their interests. From ancient ruins to castles and historic estates, these locations can serve as breathtaking backdrops for their special day.

Finally, for those planning a historical-themed wedding reception, incorporating entertainment with a historical twist can create a memorable experience for guests. From period-inspired music and dances to interactive historical games, the possibilities are endless.

In conclusion, LGBTQ+ wedding traditions and rituals have a rich and diverse history. By exploring and incorporating these elements into modern weddings, historians, and enthusiasts can celebrate the resilience, love, and commitment of LGBTQ+ couples throughout time.

Creating Inclusive Historical Wedding Spaces

When it comes to planning historical-themed weddings, it is crucial to ensure that the space is inclusive and accommodating to all guests. By creating an inclusive historical wedding space, you not only pay homage to the past but also celebrate diversity and create a memorable experience for everyone involved.

One way to achieve inclusivity is by incorporating LGBTQ+ historical weddings into the narrative. The Wedding Between Nero and Sporo is a perfect example of an ancient same-sex union and can serve as inspiration for LGBTQ+ couples seeking to honor their history. By highlighting the love story of Nero and Sporo, historians can shed light on LGBTQ+ relationships in the past while also providing a supportive and inclusive environment for modern couples.

Furthermore, unique wedding venues for historical enthusiasts can be a great way to engage guests and immerse them in the experience. Whether it's a Roman amphitheater or a medieval castle, selecting a venue that reflects the theme of the wedding can transport guests to a different era. This not only adds to the overall ambiance but also allows for a more authentic and inclusive experience.

Ancient Roman wedding traditions and rituals can also be incorporated into the ceremony to enhance the historical aspect of the event. From the exchange of rings to the lighting of a unity candle, these rituals can connect modern couples to their historical counterparts. By explaining the significance of these traditions, historians can create a deeper understanding and appreciation of the past.

Additionally, historical wedding attire and fashion play a vital role in creating an inclusive historical wedding space. By offering a diverse range of options, couples can choose attire that both reflects the historical period and embraces their personal style. This inclusivity allows individuals from various backgrounds to feel represented and celebrated.

To capture the essence of the historical wedding, photography and videography must be approached with a historical lens. Utilizing techniques and aesthetics from the past can transport guests back in time and create a truly immersive experience. By working with professionals who specialize in historical weddings, couples can ensure that their memories are preserved in a way that authentically reflects the theme.

Lastly, wedding reception entertainment with a historical twist can be a delightful addition to any historical-themed wedding. From period-specific music to historical reenactments, incorporating entertainment that aligns with the theme creates an engaging and memorable experience for guests.

Creating inclusive historical wedding spaces is not only about celebrating the past but also about embracing diversity and creating a welcoming environment for all. By incorporating LGBTQ+ historical weddings, unique venues, ancient traditions, diverse fashion choices, historical photography and videography, and entertaining with a historical twist, historians can help couples create an inclusive and unforgettable wedding experience that bridges the gap between the past and the present.

Chapter 6: Unique Wedding Venues for Historical Enthusiasts

Unconventional Historical Wedding Venues

When planning a wedding, couples often seek unique and memorable venues that reflect their interests and passions. For historians and enthusiasts of historical events, there is an entire world of unconventional wedding venues waiting to be explored. From ancient ruins to historic landmarks, these venues provide the perfect backdrop for a wedding that pays homage to the past.

Imagine exchanging vows in the very place where Nero and Sporo, two prominent figures of the Roman Empire, shared their love story. The Wedding Between Nero and Sporo: A Historical Love Story offers a glimpse into their lives and the extraordinary events that unfolded during their time. Historians, especially those fascinated by the Roman Empire, will find this subchapter particularly intriguing.

For lovers of historical reenactments, this subchapter delves into wedding planning for historical themed weddings. It provides inspiration and guidance on how to recreate the ambiance and traditions of ancient Rome. From Roman-inspired wedding themes to LGBTQ+ historical weddings, this subchapter explores the various ways historical events can be incorporated into a modern-day celebration of love.

One key aspect of any historical-themed wedding is the attire and fashion. This subchapter delves into the intricacies of historical wedding attire, offering insights into the fashions of the past. From togas to elegant Roman-inspired gowns, historians will find a wealth of inspiration for their own unique wedding attire.

Of course, no wedding is complete without photography and videography to capture those precious moments. Historical wedding photography and videography is a niche that combines artistic skill with a deep appreciation for history. This subchapter dives into the techniques and styles that can be employed to create stunning visual memories that transport couples and their guests back in time.

To complete the historical experience, the subchapter explores historical wedding favors, decorations, and entertainment. Imagine guests being entertained by gladiators or indulging in Roman delicacies during the reception. With the right attention to detail, a historical wedding can transport guests to another era and create an unforgettable experience.

For historians and those with a passion for the past, unconventional historical wedding venues offer a unique opportunity to celebrate love in a way that is truly extraordinary. Whether it's exchanging vows in ancient ruins or recreating the traditions of a bygone era, this subchapter provides inspiration and guidance for planning a wedding that will leave a lasting impression on guests and create cherished memories for the couple tying the knot.

Historic Castles and Palaces as Wedding Venues

For historians and enthusiasts of all things historical, the idea of getting married in a majestic castle or a breathtaking palace is a dream come true. The allure of these iconic buildings, steeped in rich history, adds a touch of magic and romance to any wedding ceremony. In this subchapter, we will explore the charm and significance of historic castles and palaces as wedding venues, and delve into the various aspects that make them truly exceptional choices for couples seeking a unique and memorable experience.

Imagine exchanging vows in the very same spaces where kings and queens once resided, where grand banquets and extravagant balls were held. These architectural marvels not only provide a stunning backdrop for your special day but also transport you and your guests back in time. From opulent ballrooms adorned with intricate chandeliers to magnificent gardens filled with fragrant blooms, every corner of these venues exudes grandeur and elegance.

The Wedding Between Nero and Sporo, a historical love story that captivated the ancient world, serves as an inspiration for couples seeking a historical-themed wedding. These venues offer the perfect settings to recreate the lavishness and opulence of the Roman Empire. Imagine donning ancient Roman-inspired attire, complete with flowing togas and intricate golden accessories, as you exchange your vows in a breathtaking courtyard or a regal hall.

LGBTQ+ couples can also find solace in historic castles and palaces as wedding venues. These venues, with their rich histories, often symbolize progress and acceptance. They provide a welcoming space for couples to celebrate their love and commitment, while also honoring LGBTQ+ historical figures who fought for equality and freedom.

A historical wedding wouldn't be complete without embracing ancient Roman wedding traditions and rituals. From the ceremonial processions to the symbolic tying of the knot, these customs can add a captivating touch to your special day. Capture these extraordinary moments with historical wedding photography and videography, ensuring that every detail is preserved for generations to come.

To enhance the historical ambiance, consider incorporating unique wedding favors and decorations that pay homage to the era. From Roman-inspired keepsakes to ancient artifacts, these mementos will transport your guests to a bygone era.

Lastly, for a truly unforgettable wedding reception, entertain your guests with historical performances. From reenactments of famous battles to traditional dances and music, these captivating spectacles will leave your guests in awe and create lasting memories.

In conclusion, historic castles and palaces offer an enchanting and extraordinary experience for couples seeking a wedding venue with a historical twist. Whether you are a history buff or simply appreciate the grandeur and romance of the past, these venues provide the perfect backdrop for a wedding that will be remembered for centuries to come. So, step back in time and create your own unique love story in a setting that echoes the grandeur and beauty of history.

Historical Sites and Museums for Wedding Ceremonies

For historians and enthusiasts of historical-themed weddings, finding the perfect venue to celebrate your special day can be a challenging task. However, there is a wide array of historical sites and museums that offer unique and unforgettable settings for wedding ceremonies. In this subchapter, we will explore some of the most captivating locations that will transport you and your guests back in time.

One of the most iconic historical sites for wedding ceremonies is the Colosseum in Rome. Imagine exchanging vows in the same arena where gladiators once fought for their lives, surrounded by the grandeur of ancient Roman architecture. The Colosseum offers a truly majestic backdrop for couples who want to pay homage to the Roman Empire and its rich history.

Another remarkable option is the Louvre Museum in Paris, known for its stunning architecture and extensive collection of artworks. Imagine saying "I do" in the presence of masterpieces such as the Mona Lisa or the Winged Victory of Samothrace. The Louvre's grandeur and cultural significance make it an ideal location for couples who seek a wedding venue that embodies elegance and historical allure.

For those interested in LGBTQ+ historical weddings, the Stonewall Inn in New York City holds a special place in history as the birthplace of the modern LGBTQ+ rights movement. A wedding ceremony at this iconic site would not only celebrate love and commitment but also honor the struggles and triumphs of the LGBTQ+ community throughout history.

To add a touch of ancient Roman tradition to your wedding, consider hosting your ceremony at the ruins of Pompeii. The preserved remains of this ancient city provide a unique and romantic setting, allowing you to immerse yourself in the customs and rituals of the Roman Empire. Imagine walking down the aisle amidst the crumbling ruins, surrounded by the echoes of a bygone era.

In addition to these historical sites, museums dedicated to specific periods or themes can offer an intimate and immersive experience for your wedding ceremony. For example, the Victoria and Albert Museum in London showcases a vast collection of historical fashion and decorative arts, making it an ideal venue for couples interested in historical wedding attire and fashion. Similarly, the National Museum of Natural History in Washington, D.C., offers a range of fascinating exhibits that can inspire unique wedding favors and decorations.

When it comes to planning a historical-themed wedding, the possibilities are endless. From ancient Roman traditions to LGBTQ+ historical celebrations, there are countless ways to infuse historical elements into your special day. By choosing a historical site or museum as your wedding venue, you not only create a memorable experience for yourselves and your guests but also pay tribute to the rich tapestry of history that has shaped our world. So, embrace the allure of the past and let your love story become a part of history.

Chapter 7: Ancient Roman Wedding Traditions and Rituals

The Role of Marriage in Ancient Rome

Marriage held a significant place in the social fabric of ancient Rome, playing a pivotal role in the lives of its citizens. This subchapter delves into the intricate customs, traditions, and beliefs surrounding marriage in this fascinating era.

In ancient Rome, marriage was considered a fundamental institution that served various purposes. It not only solidified alliances between families but also played a crucial role in the continuation of the Roman lineage. The primary aim of marriage was procreation, as the Romans believed it was their duty to produce offspring to ensure the survival and prosperity of their society.

Marriages in ancient Rome were often arranged, with the consent of both families being of utmost importance. Love and compatibility were secondary considerations, as the union was primarily viewed as a means of strengthening familial and political ties. This aspect of marriage was particularly prominent among the aristocracy, where strategic alliances were essential for maintaining power and influence.

Wedding ceremonies in ancient Rome were elaborate affairs, filled with rituals and traditions that symbolized the transition from singlehood to married life. One such ritual was the exchange of vows, where the couple would make promises to each other and the gods. This act was witnessed by family and friends, who often showered the couple with blessings and good wishes for their future.

The attire and fashion of the bride and groom during ancient Roman weddings were elaborate and ornate, reflecting the wealth and status of their families. The bride would typically wear a flamboyant white gown, adorned with intricate jewelry and a veil, while the groom would opt for a traditional toga, symbolizing his Roman citizenship.

Historical wedding photography and videography have become increasingly popular among modern couples seeking unique and meaningful ways to document their special day. The subchapter explores how couples can incorporate ancient Roman elements into their wedding photography and videography, capturing the essence of the era and creating everlasting memories.

For those interested in hosting historical-themed weddings, the subchapter also offers insights into unique wedding venues that can transport guests back in time. From ancient Roman villas to historic landmarks, these locations provide the perfect backdrop for couples seeking an immersive experience.

In conclusion, the role of marriage in ancient Rome was multifaceted, serving as a means of establishing alliances, ensuring the continuity of lineage, and upholding societal norms. This subchapter provides a comprehensive exploration of the customs, traditions, and significance of marriage in ancient Rome, catering to historians and niches interested in the historical, cultural, and aesthetic aspects of Roman weddings.

Ancient Roman Engagement and Betrothal Customs

In the realm of ancient Rome, engagement and betrothal customs were rich in tradition and symbolism, playing a crucial role in the lives of couples preparing for marriage. The elaborate rituals and traditions surrounding engagements in ancient Rome were not only a display of love and commitment but also served as a means to solidify alliances and secure the future of families.

Engagement in ancient Rome was a formal agreement between the families of the bride and groom-to-be. This agreement was typically arranged by the parents, who would negotiate the terms and conditions of the union. Once both families reached an agreement, the couple would be officially engaged.

One of the most significant engagement customs in ancient Rome was the exchange of betrothal gifts. These gifts, known as "arrhae," were usually given by the groom to his bride-to-be. The arrhae consisted of a ring or a piece of jewelry, symbolizing the groom's commitment to the bride. It also served as a token of the groom's financial capability to support his future wife.

Another prominent aspect of Roman engagement customs was the ceremony known as "spousalia." During this ceremony, the couple would exchange vows and promise their love and fidelity to one another. The spousalia was often accompanied by a feast, where both families would come together to celebrate the upcoming union.

Interestingly, ancient Roman engagements were legally binding, and breaking off an engagement was not taken lightly. However, if either party wished to dissolve the engagement, they could seek a legal act called "repudium." This act required the presence of witnesses and involved the return of the betrothal gifts.

Ancient Roman engagement and betrothal customs continue to inspire modern-day couples, particularly those seeking historical-themed weddings. From incorporating Roman-inspired wedding attire to reenacting traditional engagement ceremonies, the allure of ancient Rome adds a unique touch to weddings.

For historians and enthusiasts of ancient Rome, these customs provide an opportunity to delve into the rich tapestry of the past. Through historical reenactments and meticulously designed wedding venues, couples can transport themselves and their guests back in time to experience the grandeur of Roman culture firsthand.

Furthermore, the significance of LGBTQ+ historical weddings cannot be overlooked. In ancient Rome, same-sex marriages were not uncommon, and exploring this aspect of Roman history can contribute to a more inclusive understanding of love and commitment.

For those planning historical-themed weddings, attention to detail is paramount. From meticulously crafted Roman-inspired wedding attire to historically accurate photography and videography, every aspect of the wedding should reflect the beauty and elegance of ancient Rome.

In conclusion, ancient Roman engagement and betrothal customs offer a wealth of inspiration and historical significance for those interested in exploring the intricacies of the past. Whether historians, wedding planners, or couples seeking a unique wedding experience, the customs of ancient Rome provide a captivating backdrop for love, commitment, and celebration.

The Wedding Ceremony: Ancient Roman Style

In this subchapter, we delve into the fascinating world of ancient Roman wedding ceremonies. Historians and enthusiasts of historical-themed weddings will find this exploration of the wedding traditions and rituals of the Roman Empire both enlightening and inspiring. From the unique wedding venues to the historical wedding favors and decorations, we uncover the secrets of creating a truly unforgettable wedding experience.

The Roman Empire was known for its grandeur and opulence, and their wedding ceremonies were no exception. The bride and groom would exchange vows in front of family and friends, with the ceremony often taking place in a public space such as a temple or the home of a prominent citizen. Roman weddings were seen as a social event, and it was not uncommon for hundreds of guests to attend.

One of the most distinctive aspects of a Roman wedding was the role of the flamen dialis, a high priest who oversaw the ceremony. The flamen dialis would perform the sacred rituals and invoke the blessings of the gods on the couple. These rituals included the exchange of rings, the lighting of a sacred fire, and the offering of sacrifices to the gods.

When it came to attire, Roman brides would wear a white tunic known as a tunica recta, which symbolized purity and fertility. The groom would don a white toga praetexta, a garment reserved for high-ranking officials. Historical reenactment weddings can recreate these ancient fashions, allowing couples to step back in time and experience the splendor of an ancient Roman wedding.

Capturing the essence of an ancient Roman wedding requires more than just the right attire. Historical wedding photography and videography can help bring the event to life, capturing the emotions and details of the ceremony for generations to come. Additionally, couples can incorporate Roman-inspired decorations and favors, such as laurel wreaths, ancient coins, and themed centerpieces, to transport their guests to the Roman Empire.

To add a touch of excitement to the wedding reception, couples can consider entertainment with a historical twist. From gladiator fights to ancient Roman games, there are countless ways to keep guests entertained and engaged throughout the celebration.

For LGBTQ+ couples interested in historical weddings, the ancient Roman Empire offers a unique perspective. Same-sex unions were not uncommon in ancient Rome, and exploring these historical precedents can provide inspiration and validation for modern-day love stories.

Whether you're a historian or simply a lover of all things historical, an ancient Roman-themed wedding promises to be an extraordinary experience. From the ceremony rituals to the intricate details of attire, photography, and decorations, embracing the traditions of the Roman Empire can create a wedding celebration unlike any other.

Ancient Roman Wedding Feasts and Celebrations

In the grand tapestry of history, few events are as captivating as the ancient Roman wedding feasts and celebrations. These extravagant spectacles were filled with opulence, luxury, and a unique blend of traditions and rituals that have left an indelible mark on the annals of time.

In the subchapter titled "Ancient Roman Wedding Feasts and Celebrations," we delve into the captivating world of these historical love stories, exploring the rich tapestry of customs and practices that adorned these occasions.

For historians and enthusiasts of the Roman Empire, this subchapter is a treasure trove of knowledge. Discover the intricacies of planning weddings that echo the opulence and grandeur of ancient Rome. From the lavish decorations to the sumptuous feasts that adorned these celebrations, every detail is meticulously explored.

Immerse yourself in the world of historical reenactment weddings as we unveil the secrets behind recreating the splendor of an ancient Roman wedding. From the choice of venue to the attire worn by the couple and guests, we leave no stone unturned in our quest to provide an authentic experience.

Explore the unique wedding venues that cater to the desires of historical enthusiasts. From ancient ruins to grand villas, these sites offer the perfect backdrop for a love story that transcends time.

Delve into the ancient Roman wedding traditions and rituals that have stood the test of time. Uncover the significance of the sacred rites, such as the exchanging of rings and the lighting of the sacred fire, and understand how they were woven into the fabric of these celebrations.

Witness the evolution of historical wedding attire and fashion as we transport you back in time to an era of flowing togas, intricate hairstyles, and ornate jewelry. Marvel at the beauty and elegance of these garments, and gain inspiration for your own Roman Empire-inspired wedding theme.

Capture the essence of these historical weddings with the help of skilled photographers and videographers who specialize in capturing the magic of the past. Learn about the techniques and styles employed to ensure that every precious moment is immortalized.

Complete the experience with historical wedding favors and decorations that transport your guests to the ancient Roman world. From intricate mosaics to delicately crafted pottery, these keepsakes will serve as a testament to the timeless romance that unfolds on your special day.

Finally, entertain your guests with a historical twist at the wedding reception. From gladiator battles to ancient Roman dance performances, these unique forms of entertainment will transport your guests to a bygone era, leaving them mesmerized and captivated.

In "Ancient Roman Wedding Feasts and Celebrations," we invite you to embark on a journey through time, where love, tradition, and opulence intertwine to create a truly unforgettable experience. Join us as we unveil the secrets of the past and celebrate the eternal union between Nero and Sporo, a love story that transcends time itself.

Chapter 8: Historical Wedding Attire and Fashion

Researching and Recreating Historical Wedding Attire

When planning a historical themed wedding, one of the most exciting aspects is researching and recreating the attire of the era. For historians and enthusiasts of the past, the opportunity to delve into the fashion of a bygone era and bring it to life in a modern-day wedding is truly enchanting.

In the case of the wedding between Nero and Sporo, set in the Roman Empire, the task of researching and recreating historical wedding attire is both challenging and rewarding. The Roman Empire was known for its elaborate and exquisite fashion, and the wedding attire of the time was no exception.

To accurately recreate the historical wedding attire, historians and wedding planners must first embark on a thorough research journey. This involves studying ancient texts, paintings, and artifacts that provide insights into the fashion trends of the Roman Empire. Understanding the fabrics, silhouettes, and embellishments of the era is crucial in creating authentic attire.

Once the research phase is complete, the next step is to recreate the attire. This often involves collaborating with skilled costume designers and seamstresses who specialize in historical fashion. These experts can bring the vision to life by meticulously crafting each garment, paying attention to every intricate detail.

For a wedding inspired by the Roman Empire, the bride's attire could feature a flowing white tunic, known as a stola, adorned with intricate gold embroidery. The groom might don a regal purple toga, symbolizing his status and wealth. These outfits would be accessorized with authentic Roman jewelry, such as gold bracelets and laurel wreaths.

Capturing the essence of historical wedding attire is not only important for the couple but also for the wedding photography and videography. Hiring professionals experienced in capturing historical themes ensures that every detail is documented, allowing the couple to relive the magic of their special day for years to come.

To complete the immersive experience, the wedding reception entertainment can also be infused with a historical twist. From traditional Roman dance performances to reenactments of ancient wedding rituals, guests will be transported back in time and immersed in the rich culture of the Roman Empire.

For those planning a historical themed wedding, researching and recreating historical wedding attire is a fascinating journey. By paying homage to the past and embracing the traditions of bygone eras, couples can create a truly unique and memorable wedding experience that will be cherished for a lifetime.

Ancient Roman Wedding Attire and Accessories

When it comes to ancient Roman weddings, the attire and accessories worn by the bride and groom were of utmost importance. These garments not only represented their social status but also played a significant role in the overall aesthetics of the ceremony. In this subchapter, we will explore the fascinating world of ancient Roman wedding attire and accessories.

For the bride, the wedding dress was a symbol of purity and modesty. It typically consisted of a long, flowing white tunic called a "tunica recta," which was made of fine linen or silk. Over this, she would wear a colorful bridal veil known as a "flammeum," which was often yellow or orange.

The flammeum was believed to ward off evil spirits and protect the bride from any potential harm.

To complete her ensemble, the bride would adorn herself with various accessories. A golden wreath, known as a "sagina," was placed on her head as a symbol of her marital status. She would also wear a necklace, earrings, and bracelets made of precious gemstones, such as pearls, emeralds, or rubies. These accessories not only added a touch of elegance but also showcased the wealth and status of the bride's family.

The groom, on the other hand, would wear a white toga called a "toga virilis." This garment symbolized his transition from adolescence to adulthood and was considered a mark of his citizenship and social standing. The toga virilis was often adorned with purple stripes, which were reserved for the highest-ranking officials and aristocrats.

In addition to the toga, the groom would wear a golden or silver belt known as a "cingulum." This belt not only held the toga in place but also served as a symbol of his authority and power. To complete his wedding attire, the groom would wear a wreath made of myrtle leaves, which was believed to bring good fortune and fertility.

To capture the beauty and grandeur of these ancient Roman weddings, it was common for couples to hire skilled photographers and videographers. These professionals would use traditional techniques and equipment to create stunning images and videos that would be cherished for generations.

Furthermore, couples who wished to incorporate historical elements into their modern-day weddings could opt for unique venues that resembled ancient Roman architecture. From magnificent gardens to opulent banquet halls, these venues provided the perfect backdrop for a Roman empire-inspired celebration.

Whether it's through historical reenactments, LGBTQ+ historical weddings, or themed wedding planning, the allure of ancient Roman wedding attire and accessories continues to captivate historians and wedding enthusiasts alike. So, delve into the world of ancient Rome and let your imagination run wild as you plan your own historical love story.

Historical Hairstyles and Makeup for Weddings

Historians have always been fascinated by the intricate details of historical events, and weddings are no exception. A wedding is not only a celebration of love but also a reflection of the traditions and customs of a specific era. In this subchapter, we delve into the world of historical hairstyles and makeup for weddings, exploring the fascinating styles and trends that have emerged throughout the ages.

When it comes to historical themed weddings, the hair and makeup play a crucial role in creating an authentic atmosphere. For a wedding inspired by the love story between Nero and Sporo, one could recreate the extravagant hairstyles of ancient Rome. The Roman women were known for their elaborate updos adorned with intricate braids, jeweled hairpins, and even fresh flowers. To achieve the perfect Roman look, hairstylists can use modern techniques combined with historical references, resulting in a stunning and unique hairstyle for the bride.

Makeup in ancient Rome was characterized by a pale complexion, flushed cheeks, and bold eyes. Historians can recreate this look by using natural ingredients such as crushed berries for blush and charcoal for eyeliner. Adding authenticity to the makeup will transport the couple and their guests back in time, immersing them in the rich history of the Roman Empire.

For LGBTQ+ historical weddings, historical hairstyles and makeup can be a powerful way to honor the struggles and achievements of the community throughout history. From the flamboyant hairstyles of the

Renaissance to the androgynous styles of the 1920s, LGBTQ+ couples have the opportunity to express themselves authentically while celebrating their love in a historical context.

When planning a historical themed wedding, it is essential to consider the venue and decorations. The choice of location can greatly enhance the overall experience, allowing the couple and their guests to truly feel as if they have stepped back in time. Historical venues such as castles, manors, or even ancient ruins provide the perfect backdrop for a romantic and immersive experience.

To capture the essence of a historical wedding, couples can hire photographers and videographers specialized in historical reenactments. These professionals have the expertise to recreate the atmosphere of the chosen era, employing unique lighting techniques and artistic direction to immortalize the special day in a way that is both beautiful and historically accurate.

In conclusion, historical hairstyles and makeup for weddings offer an exciting opportunity to transport couples and their guests back in time. Whether inspired by the Roman Empire, LGBTQ+ history, or any other era, historical themed weddings provide a unique and memorable experience for everyone involved. From the elaborate hairstyles to the authentic makeup, every detail contributes to creating a wedding that is both historically accurate and deeply meaningful.

The Influence of Historical Fashion on Modern Wedding Dresses

Throughout history, fashion has always played a significant role in society, reflecting the values, traditions, and cultural norms of a particular era. When it comes to weddings, the influence of historical fashion is undeniable. From ancient Rome to the modern-day, the evolution of wedding dresses has been shaped by the trends and styles of the past.

In "The Wedding Between Nero and Sporo: A Historical Love Story," we explore the captivating world of historical weddings and the impact they have had on modern wedding dresses. Historians and enthusiasts of historical-themed weddings will find this subchapter particularly intriguing as we delve into the fascinating connection between past and present.

Ancient Rome, with its opulence and grandeur, serves as an excellent starting point for exploring historical wedding attire. Roman-inspired wedding themes have become increasingly popular, with couples embracing the luxurious fabrics, intricate draping, and regal silhouettes reminiscent of this ancient empire. We delve into the details of Roman wedding traditions and rituals, shedding light on the symbolism behind specific garments and accessories.

For LGBTQ+ couples interested in historical weddings, we explore how same-sex unions were celebrated throughout different time periods. From ancient Greece to Renaissance Europe, we uncover stories of love and commitment, providing inspiration for today's LGBTQ+ couples who wish to honor their history through their wedding celebrations.

Unique wedding venues for historical enthusiasts are also a key aspect of this subchapter. From majestic castles to ancient ruins, we showcase extraordinary locations that provide the perfect backdrop for couples seeking a truly immersive historical experience.

Of course, no historical wedding would be complete without the finer details. We explore historical wedding favors and decorations, highlighting the significance of specific motifs and materials. Additionally, we delve into the world of historical wedding photography and videography, discussing techniques that capture the essence of a bygone era.

Finally, for those seeking entertainment with a historical twist, we discuss unique wedding reception ideas inspired by different time periods. From medieval feasts to Victorian-era dances, we provide inspiration for couples looking to create an unforgettable experience for their guests.

"The Influence of Historical Fashion on Modern Wedding Dresses" is a captivating subchapter that caters to historians and enthusiasts of historical-themed weddings. By exploring the connection between past and present, we celebrate the rich tapestry of history and its impact on one of life's most joyous occasions.

Chapter 9: Historical Wedding Photography and Videography

Capturing the Essence of History in Wedding Photos

Wedding photos are not just mere snapshots; they are a timeless documentation of a couple's love and commitment. For historians, capturing the essence of history in wedding photos goes beyond the traditional poses and smiles. It is about creating images that transport us back in time, allowing us to experience the beauty and grandeur of historical periods, customs, and traditions. In this subchapter, we delve into the art of preserving history through wedding photography and explore how to make your special day a historical masterpiece.

The Wedding Between Nero and Sporo: A Historical Love Story, serves as the inspiration for this exploration. This epic love story, set in the Roman Empire, offers a rich tapestry of historical themes and elements that can be incorporated into wedding planning. From the attire and fashion of the era to the ancient Roman wedding traditions and rituals, every detail can be meticulously recreated to ensure an authentic historical experience.

One of the key elements in capturing the essence of history lies in choosing the right location. Historical enthusiasts seek unique wedding venues that transport them to a bygone era. From ancient ruins to grand palaces, these venues provide the perfect backdrop for historical reenactment weddings. Imagine exchanging vows amidst the iconic monuments of the Roman Empire or in a beautifully restored Roman villa.

To add an LGBTQ+ twist to historical weddings, we explore how same-sex couples can incorporate their unique love stories into the historical narrative. By highlighting LGBTQ+ historical figures and their relationships, we can celebrate love and equality throughout history.

Wedding photography and videography play a crucial role in immortalizing the historical charm of the event. By employing techniques such as sepia tones, vintage filters, and dramatic lighting, photographers can transport us into a different era. They can capture the intricate details of historical wedding attire, the beauty of ancient traditions, and the emotions that are evoked during these moments.

Historical wedding favors and decorations are another essential aspect of creating an immersive experience. From Roman coin souvenirs to ancient-inspired table centerpieces, every detail can contribute to the historical ambiance. Moreover, incorporating historical reception entertainment, such as period music or dance performances, adds an interactive element that enhances the overall experience for guests.

In conclusion, capturing the essence of history in wedding photos allows us to transcend time and celebrate love through the lens of the past. Whether it is through historical wedding planning, ancient traditions, or LGBTQ+ narratives, historians and enthusiasts can create unforgettable experiences that blend the beauty of the present with the allure of the past. So, embrace the historical charm, and let your wedding become a masterpiece that tells a story for generations to come.

Working with Historical Props and Settings

In the mesmerizing world of historical weddings, attention to detail is everything. From the grandeur of ancient Rome to the allure of LGBTQ+ historical love stories, this subchapter explores the fascinating realm of working with historical props and settings for an unforgettable wedding experience.

For the historians and enthusiasts of "The Wedding Between Nero and Sporo," this subchapter is a treasure trove of inspiration. Dive into the intricacies of wedding planning for historical themed weddings and discover the secrets behind crafting the perfect Roman empire-inspired wedding theme.

Immerse yourself in the captivating world of historical reenactment weddings, where couples can recreate historical events with meticulous accuracy. Explore the ancient Roman wedding traditions and rituals, and learn how to incorporate them into modern ceremonies, creating a beautiful blend of the old and the new.

As historians, capturing the essence of the past is paramount. Discover the art of historical wedding attire and fashion, from the Roman togas and tunics to the elaborate costumes of different eras. Learn how to select the perfect attire for a historical-themed wedding, ensuring authenticity and elegance.

No historical wedding is complete without capturing the memories through photography and videography. Uncover the secrets of capturing the essence of love in a historical setting, creating timeless images that transport couples back in time.

Delve into the world of historical wedding favors and decorations, where every detail plays a significant role in recreating historical eras. From ancient Roman-inspired trinkets to personalized tokens of love, discover unique ways to delight guests and create a truly immersive experience.

Take your guests on a journey through time with wedding reception entertainment with a historical twist. From enchanting musicians playing ancient melodies to captivating storytelling performances, create an unforgettable atmosphere that transports everyone to a bygone era.

Finally, explore unique wedding venues for historical enthusiasts, from ancient ruins and castles to historical landmarks. Discover hidden gems that offer the perfect backdrop for a historical-themed wedding, creating an unforgettable experience for the couple and their guests.

Whether you are a historian, a couple planning a unique wedding, or an LGBTQ+ individual seeking to celebrate love through historical reenactment, this subchapter is your guide to creating an extraordinary wedding experience. Let history become the muse that weaves a love story for the ages.

Incorporating Vintage Techniques into Wedding Photography

Weddings have always been a celebration of love and a reflection of the times. For historians and enthusiasts of historical weddings, capturing the essence of a bygone era is an essential part of the experience. In this subchapter, we will explore the art of incorporating vintage techniques into wedding photography, allowing couples to relive the magic of the past on their special day.

One of the most captivating aspects of vintage photography is the use of film. By embracing traditional film cameras, photographers can create a timeless and nostalgic feel in their images. The softness, texture, and grain of film add a unique character that cannot be replicated with digital photography. For historians and lovers of all things ancient, this technique can transport them back in time, capturing the essence of historical wedding themes.

Another technique that can be employed is hand-tinting. This technique, popularized in the early 20th century, involves meticulously applying color to black and white photographs. By selectively adding hues to specific elements of the image, photographers can create a stunning effect that evokes the romance and charm of vintage photographs. Hand-tinted wedding portraits are not only visually striking but also serve as cherished heirlooms that can be passed down through generations.

In addition to film and hand-tinting, photographers can experiment with vintage lenses and equipment. These tools offer a distinct aesthetic, with unique characteristics such as vignetting, soft focus, and flares. By using vintage lenses, photographers can transport viewers back to a time when these imperfections were embraced and celebrated.

To truly capture the essence of historical weddings, photographers can also explore alternative printing methods. Processes such as cyanotype, albumen, and platinum printing produce beautifully textured and timeless images. These methods, rooted in the early days of photography, add an extra layer of authenticity to the final prints.

Incorporating vintage techniques into wedding photography allows couples to create a visual narrative that is not only stunning but also deeply meaningful. By embracing the artistry and craftsmanship of the past, photographers can transport viewers to a different era, capturing the essence of historical themes and traditions. Whether it's a Roman empire-inspired wedding or an LGBTQ+ historical celebration, vintage photography techniques offer a unique way to honor the past while celebrating love in the present.

Creating Timeless Wedding Videos with a Historical Touch

In the world of wedding videography, capturing the essence and beauty of a couple's special day is of utmost importance. But what if you could take it a step further and infuse historical elements into the video, adding a touch of timelessness and enchantment? This subchapter explores the art of creating wedding videos with a historical touch, perfect for those interested in the love story between Nero and Sporo, as well as historians and enthusiasts of historical-themed weddings.

One of the key aspects of creating a timeless wedding video is to incorporate the historical backdrop in a subtle yet impactful manner. Whether it be a Roman empire-inspired wedding theme or a LGBTQ+ historical wedding, the video should transport viewers back in time, immersing them in the rich historical atmosphere. This can be achieved through careful selection of wedding venues that reflect the chosen historical era, such as ancient ruins or historical landmarks.

To further enhance the historical touch, it is essential to weave in elements of ancient Roman wedding traditions and rituals. From the sacred exchange of vows to the symbolic breaking of bread, these customs add depth and meaning to the video, creating a connection between the past and the present. Additionally, showcasing the historical wedding attire and fashion of the era adds a visual feast for the viewers, immersing them in the beauty and elegance of the past.

Another crucial factor in creating a timeless wedding video is the selection of a skilled videographer who understands the significance of capturing every moment with precision and artistry. The videographer should possess a deep appreciation for history and a keen eye for capturing the unique details that define a historical-themed wedding. By incorporating cinematic techniques and editing styles that mirror the aesthetics of the chosen era, the resulting video will be a true work of art.

Lastly, to add an extra layer of authenticity, historical wedding favors and decorations can be integrated into the video. From ancient Roman coins to handmade trinkets reminiscent of the past, these small details contribute to the overall historical ambiance.

Whether you are a historian, a couple planning a historical-themed wedding, or simply an enthusiast of all things historical, creating timeless wedding videos with a historical touch is a captivating way to celebrate love and history. With careful attention to detail and a passion for storytelling, these videos will not only capture the essence of the couple's special day but also transport viewers on a journey through time.

Chapter 10: Historical Wedding Favors and Decorations

Selecting Historical-inspired Wedding Favors

When planning a wedding with a historical theme, every detail matters, including the wedding favors. These small tokens of appreciation are an opportunity to transport your guests back in time and create a unique and memorable experience. In this subchapter, we will explore different ideas and inspirations for selecting historical-inspired wedding favors that will delight your guests and add an authentic touch to your special day.

One option for historical-inspired wedding favors is to incorporate elements from the wedding's time period or theme. For example, if you are planning a Roman Empire-inspired wedding, consider gifting miniature replicas of ancient Roman artifacts, such as coins or pottery fragments. These can be beautifully displayed on a small plaque or in a velvet pouch, allowing guests to take home a piece of history.

Another idea is to choose favors inspired by the traditions and rituals of the time period. For LGBTQ+ historical weddings, you can opt for personalized rainbow-colored ribbons or badges that symbolize love and inclusivity. These favors not only celebrate your love but also honor the struggles and triumphs of the LGBTQ+ community throughout history.

If you are hosting a historical reenactment wedding, consider favors that reflect the era you are recreating. For example, for a medieval-themed wedding, you can offer small bottles of homemade mead or honey jars adorned with vintage labels. These favors will not only add authenticity to your event but also give guests a taste of the past.

Additionally, it's important to consider the presentation of your wedding favors. Use vintage-inspired packaging, such as ornate boxes or parchment envelopes, to enhance the historical feel. You can also include a small note explaining the significance of the favor and its connection to the wedding theme, providing guests with a deeper understanding and appreciation for the gesture.

In conclusion, selecting historical-inspired wedding favors is an opportunity to add a special touch to your wedding and create a unique experience for your guests. By incorporating elements from the time period or theme, as well as considering the traditions and rituals associated with it, you can choose favors that transport your guests back in time. Don't forget to pay attention to the presentation, as the packaging and accompanying note can further enhance the historical feel. Your guests will surely appreciate these thoughtful tokens and cherish the memories of your historical-themed wedding for years to come.

DIY Historical-inspired Wedding Decorations

Planning a wedding with a historical theme can be a truly unique and captivating experience. If you're a history enthusiast or simply looking for a wedding that stands out from the crowd, incorporating historical elements into your special day can create an atmosphere of enchantment and romance. In this subchapter, we will explore DIY historical-inspired wedding decorations that will transport you and your guests to a bygone era.

Ancient Roman wedding themes are particularly popular among those who are fascinated by the grandeur of the Roman Empire. From the opulent decorations to the symbolic rituals, there are countless ways to infuse your wedding with Roman charm. Consider using laurel wreaths and olive branches as centerpieces or incorporating classical columns into your venue decor. Roman-inspired statues and busts can also add a touch of elegance to your reception area.

To add a personal touch to your historical wedding, consider incorporating LGBTQ+ elements to celebrate the love story of Nero and Sporo. For instance, you can create a rainbow-colored floral arch as a backdrop for your ceremony or use rainbow-colored ribbons to decorate the chairs. These small but meaningful details will ensure that your wedding is inclusive and honors the historical significance of LGBTQ+ relationships.

When it comes to historical wedding attire, you have the opportunity to truly embrace the fashion of the era you are drawing inspiration from. For a Roman-themed wedding, consider incorporating flowing togas, intricate jewelry, and Roman-style sandals into your attire. To capture the essence of the time, opt for natural fabrics such as silk and linen in muted colors like ivory, gold, and deep red.

Capturing the essence of a historical wedding through photography and videography is essential to preserving the memories of your special day. Seek out photographers and videographers who specialize in historical reenactments to ensure that every detail is captured with authenticity and artistic flair. From sepia-toned photographs to cinematic techniques reminiscent of classic movies, these professionals will create timeless mementos that will transport you back in time.

Finally, no historical-inspired wedding would be complete without carefully selected decorations and favors. Consider incorporating small Roman coins as table centerpieces or gifting your guests with personalized wax seals. You can also create unique favors such as mini scrolls with personalized messages or miniature historical artifacts that reflect the era you have chosen.

Whether you're a history enthusiast, planning a LGBTQ+ wedding, or simply looking for a wedding that breaks away from tradition, DIY historical-inspired decorations will bring a touch of enchantment and elegance to your special day. By infusing your wedding with elements from the past, you will create an unforgettable experience for you and your guests, leaving a lasting impression for years to come.

Authentic Historical Artifacts as Wedding Decor

When it comes to planning a wedding, many couples seek to create a unique and memorable experience for themselves and their guests. For those who have a passion for history, incorporating authentic historical artifacts as wedding decor can add an extra layer of intrigue and romance to the event. In this subchapter, we will explore the various ways in which couples can infuse their love for history into their special day, specifically focusing on the wedding between Nero and Sporo.

The Wedding Between Nero and Sporo is a legendary love story that has captivated historians for centuries. By drawing inspiration from this historical event, couples can create a wedding that not only celebrates love but also pays homage to the past. From the venue to the decorations, every aspect of the wedding can be carefully curated to transport guests back in time to ancient Rome.

One of the most exciting aspects of incorporating historical artifacts into the wedding decor is the opportunity to showcase genuine pieces from the Roman Empire. Imagine walking down the aisle surrounded by ancient statues, busts, and pottery. These artifacts not only add a touch of authenticity but also serve as conversation starters for guests who are history enthusiasts themselves.

In addition to the venue decor, couples can also consider incorporating historical wedding traditions and rituals into their ceremony. From the exchanging of olive wreaths to the lighting of a unity candle, these rituals can add a deeper meaning to the wedding ceremony and create a sense of connection to the past.

Furthermore, historical wedding attire and fashion can also play a significant role in creating an authentic atmosphere. Drawing inspiration from ancient Roman fashion, couples can opt for traditional Roman-inspired wedding attire, complete with flowing togas and intricate laurel wreaths.

To capture the essence of the day, couples can also hire a professional historical wedding photographer and videographer. These experts specialize in capturing the unique charm and beauty of historical weddings, ensuring that every moment is documented for years to come.

Lastly, the wedding reception can be transformed into a truly immersive experience with historical entertainment and decorations. From live reenactments of ancient Roman dances to historical games and performances, guests will be transported back in time and will have an unforgettable experience.

For those planning a historical-themed wedding, incorporating authentic historical artifacts as wedding decor can elevate the event to a whole new level. From the venue to the attire, every aspect can be carefully curated to create a truly immersive experience that celebrates both love and history. Whether you are a historian, a lover of the Roman Empire, or simply seeking a unique wedding experience, this subchapter will guide you through the process of planning a wedding that will be remembered for centuries to come.

Creating a Cohesive Historical Atmosphere through Decor

When it comes to planning a historical-themed wedding, one of the key elements that can truly transport your guests back in time is the decor. By carefully selecting and incorporating historical elements into your wedding venue, you can create a cohesive historical atmosphere that will leave a lasting impression on your guests. In this subchapter, we will explore various ways to bring history to life through decor, ensuring that every detail reflects the era of your choice.

To begin with, let's delve into the world of ancient Rome, the backdrop of the love story between Nero and Sporo. Roman empire-inspired wedding themes are gaining popularity among couples who wish to celebrate their love in a grand, historical setting. Consider incorporating Roman architectural elements such as columns, arches, and ruins into your venue decor. These can be created using props or even projected onto walls for a realistic effect.

In addition to architectural elements, don't forget to pay attention to the smaller details that can truly elevate the historical ambiance. Ancient Roman wedding traditions and rituals can be incorporated into your ceremony, such as the exchange of coins or the tying of the knot. Historical wedding attire and fashion can also play a significant role in creating an authentic atmosphere. Encourage your guests to dress in Roman-inspired attire, and consider providing a costume rental service for those who want to fully immerse themselves in the experience.

When it comes to documenting your historical-themed wedding, hiring a professional photographer and videographer who specialize in historical weddings is essential. They will know how to capture the essence of your event, ensuring that every shot reflects the historical atmosphere you have created.

To further enhance the experience for your guests, consider incorporating historical wedding favors and decorations. These can range from Roman-inspired trinkets and tokens to personalized items that reflect the love story between Nero and Sporo. Additionally, provide wedding reception entertainment with a historical twist. This could include performances by historical reenactment groups, live musicians playing era-specific instruments, and even interactive activities for guests to immerse themselves in the historical setting.

Remember, creating a cohesive historical atmosphere through decor is all about attention to detail. By carefully selecting and incorporating historical elements, your wedding will become an unforgettable experience for both you and your guests. So, let your imagination run wild and transport your loved ones back in time to the era of Nero and Sporo's epic love story.

Chapter 11: Wedding Reception Entertainment with a Historical Twist

Historical-inspired Musical Performances

Music has always played a significant role in historical events, cultures, and traditions. From ancient civilizations to modern societies, the power of music has been harnessed to celebrate, commemorate, and express emotions. In "The Wedding Between Nero and Sporo: A Historical Love Story," the significance of historical-inspired musical performances takes center stage.

For historians and those fascinated by historical events, the subchapter on historical-inspired musical performances provides a captivating exploration of the role of music in various historical contexts. This section offers a comprehensive guide on how to incorporate historical music into weddings, particularly those with a historical theme.

Drawing inspiration from the love story of Nero and Sporo, this subchapter delves into the musical traditions of ancient Rome. It explores the various instruments and musical styles prevalent during that time, shedding light on the unique sounds and melodies that would have accompanied weddings in the Roman Empire.

For historians planning historical-themed weddings, this subchapter provides invaluable insights into selecting appropriate musical performances. It offers suggestions for choosing musicians who specialize in historical music, ensuring an authentic and immersive experience for wedding guests.

Furthermore, this subchapter explores the connection between historical-inspired music and LGBTQ+ historical weddings. By highlighting historical figures who challenged societal norms regarding gender and sexuality, it celebrates the diversity and inclusivity of love throughout history.

The subchapter also delves into the significance of historical wedding attire and fashion. It explores how music can be intertwined with the visual elements of a wedding, showcasing the symbiotic relationship between music and fashion throughout history. From ancient Roman togas to elaborate Renaissance gowns, this section offers a wealth of inspiration for couples seeking to create a historically accurate and visually stunning wedding.

Additionally, the subchapter delves into the role of historical music in wedding photography and videography. It discusses the importance of capturing the essence of historical-inspired musical performances, ensuring that these moments are immortalized in visual form.

Lastly, this subchapter explores the various forms of entertainment with a historical twist that can be incorporated into wedding receptions. From medieval-inspired minstrels to Baroque-style orchestras, it provides a range of entertainment ideas that will transport guests back in time and create an unforgettable experience.

In conclusion, the subchapter on historical-inspired musical performances in "The Wedding Between Nero and Sporo: A Historical Love Story" is a treasure trove of inspiration and guidance for historians and those interested in historical weddings. From ancient Rome to LGBTQ+ historical weddings, this section explores the rich tapestry of historical music and its ability to create an enchanting and immersive wedding experience.

Interactive Historical Games and Activities

For historians and enthusiasts of historical-themed weddings, there is a world of interactive historical games and activities waiting to be explored. These games and activities not only provide entertainment but also offer a unique opportunity to immerse oneself in the rich history of the past. Whether you are planning a wedding with a Roman Empire-inspired theme or simply seeking to add a historical twist to your reception, these interactive experiences are sure to captivate and delight.

One popular game that can be enjoyed by guests of all ages is a historical scavenger hunt. Set the stage by creating a list of historically significant items or landmarks that guests must find throughout the wedding venue. This not only encourages exploration but also educates participants on the historical context behind each item. As guests hunt for artifacts or clues, they will uncover fascinating insights into the world of ancient Rome, LGBTQ+ historical events, or any other historical period of interest.

Another engaging activity is a historical trivia contest. Create a list of questions related to the topic of your wedding, such as ancient Roman wedding traditions, LGBTQ+ historical figures, or even historical fashion. Guests can form teams and compete for prizes while expanding their knowledge of history. This game can be tailored to fit any historical theme and is an excellent way to encourage friendly competition and learning.

For those who wish to step back in time, consider incorporating historical reenactment activities into your wedding reception. Hire professional actors or enthusiasts to portray historical figures, such as Emperor Nero and his beloved Sporo, and have them interact with guests. This immersive experience will transport your guests to another era and provide an unforgettable memory for everyone involved.

To capture the essence of your historical-themed wedding, consider setting up a photo booth with historically accurate props and costumes. Guests can dress up as Roman emperors, gladiators, or other historical characters and take memorable photographs. This not only adds a touch of fun to the celebration but also creates lasting mementos for guests to cherish.

In conclusion, interactive historical games and activities are a fantastic way to engage historians and enthusiasts attending weddings with historical themes. Whether through scavenger hunts, trivia contests, reenactments, or photo booths, these experiences provide a unique opportunity to learn, have fun, and create lasting memories. So, embrace the rich tapestry of history and make your wedding an experience that will transport guests to another time.

Historical Dance Performances

In the grand tapestry of history, dance has always played a vital role in capturing the essence of a particular era. Through graceful movements, intricate choreography, and the vibrant rhythm of music, dance has been a means of expressing emotions, celebrating milestones, and preserving cultural traditions. This subchapter delves into the captivating world of historical dance performances, offering a glimpse into the enchanting past and its influence on weddings.

For historians and lovers of history, exploring historical dance performances is like stepping into a time machine. The Wedding Between Nero and Sporo, a love story set in ancient Rome, serves as a perfect backdrop to showcase the magnificence of these dance forms. From the passionate and fiery Flamenco to the elegant and refined Waltz, each dance reveals a unique facet of history.

When it comes to wedding planning for historical themed weddings, incorporating historical dance performances adds a touch of authenticity and spectacle. Imagine a Roman empire-inspired wedding theme where professional dancers clad in ancient costumes perform traditional Roman dances, mesmerizing guests with their skill and grace.

For LGBTQ+ historical weddings, these dance performances offer a chance to celebrate love and equality through the lens of history. Historical reenactment weddings become even more immersive and memorable when dancers recreate ancient wedding rituals and perform traditional dances from the era.

Unique wedding venues for historical enthusiasts provide the perfect setting for these dance performances. From grand ballrooms to ancient ruins, the stage is set for couples to experience the magic of history through dance.

Capturing these extraordinary moments is essential, and historical wedding photography and videography play a crucial role. Skilled photographers and videographers can freeze these dance performances in time, ensuring that the beauty and significance of historical dances are preserved for generations to come.

To further enhance the historical ambiance, wedding reception entertainment can take on a historical twist. Imagine guests being entertained by professional dancers performing elaborate Renaissance dances or energetic Victorian-era reels, bringing the past to life and creating an unforgettable experience.

In conclusion, historical dance performances are a captivating art form that adds depth and authenticity to weddings. From ancient Roman wedding traditions and rituals to the mesmerizing dance movements of different eras, these performances transport us to a bygone era. Whether it is through historical wedding attire, photography, favors, decorations, or reception entertainment, embracing the beauty of historical dance performances will create an enchanting experience for historians and all those who appreciate the richness of the past.

Incorporating Historical Entertainment into the Wedding Program

When planning a wedding, couples often strive to create a memorable experience for their guests. For history enthusiasts, incorporating historical entertainment into the wedding program can add a unique and captivating element to the celebration. In this subchapter, we explore various ways to incorporate historical entertainment into your wedding, taking inspiration from the love story between Emperor Nero and his beloved Sporo.

Firstly, let's consider the wedding venue. Historical enthusiasts may opt for a Roman empire-inspired wedding theme, complete with a venue reminiscent of ancient Rome. Whether it's an elegant garden or a grand hall adorned with Roman-inspired decorations, the venue can transport guests back in time, setting the stage for an unforgettable experience.

To enhance the historical ambiance, couples can incorporate ancient Roman wedding traditions and rituals. From the exchange of rings to the lighting of a unity candle, these rituals can be modified to reflect the couple's personal preferences while maintaining a historical authenticity.

Furthermore, historical wedding attire and fashion play a significant role in immersing guests in the era. Brides may opt for elegant Roman-inspired gowns, while grooms can don traditional Roman tunics. LGBTQ+ couples can embrace historical cross-dressing traditions, mirroring the love story of Nero and Sporo.

Capturing the essence of the event with historical photography and videography is essential. Hiring professionals experienced in historical reenactments will ensure that every moment is documented with precision and artistry, preserving the memories for generations to come.

Historical wedding favors and decorations can further enhance the guest experience. Consider providing guests with personalized Roman coins or replicas of ancient artifacts as wedding favors. Additionally, incorporating historical elements into table settings and decorations can create an immersive atmosphere.

To keep guests entertained during the reception, consider unique wedding entertainment with a historical twist. From live performances of ancient Roman music to historical reenactments, there are countless ways to engage and delight your guests, making it a night to remember.

In conclusion, incorporating historical entertainment into the wedding program can create a truly exceptional experience for history enthusiasts. From the venue and attire to photography and entertainment, every aspect can be tailored to reflect the love story between Nero and Sporo, while also incorporating other historical elements. By immersing guests in the rich history of ancient Rome, couples can create a wedding celebration that is both memorable and deeply meaningful.

Conclusion:

In the pages preceding this conclusion, we have embarked on a journey through history, exploring the fascinating love story between Emperor Nero and his beloved Sporo. This historical account has shed light on the complexities of their relationship, the societal norms of ancient Rome, and the struggles faced by LGBTQ+ individuals in a time far removed from our own.

For historians, this exploration provides a valuable glimpse into the lives of Nero and Sporo, offering a deeper understanding of the Roman Empire and the dynamics of power and love within it. It is through stories like theirs that we can piece together a more comprehensive understanding of the past.

But this book is not just for historians; it is also for the wedding enthusiasts who seek to incorporate historical themes into their own special day. The tale of Nero and Sporo serves as a rich source of inspiration for those planning historically-themed weddings. From ancient Roman wedding traditions and rituals to the finest details of historical wedding attire and fashion, this book has provided a wealth of ideas to create an unforgettable event.

Moreover, the world of historical reenactment weddings opens up new and exciting possibilities. Imagine exchanging vows in an authentic Roman amphitheater, surrounded by costumed actors who bring the past to life. This subchapter has explored unique wedding venues for historical enthusiasts, offering a range of options to suit every couple's preferences.

No wedding is complete without capturing the memories in stunning photographs and videos. Historical wedding photography and videography have the power to transport couples back in time, recreating the ambiance and emotions of a bygone era. This book has delved into the techniques and styles that can be used to achieve this effect, ensuring that the memories of your special day will be cherished for generations to come.

Lastly, we have touched upon the importance of historical wedding favors and decorations, as well as the various forms of entertainment that can add a historical twist to your reception. From Roman-inspired table centerpieces to reenactment performances, these elements can truly immerse your guests in the spirit of the past, making your wedding an unforgettable experience for all.

In conclusion, "The Wedding Between Nero and Sporo: A Historical Love Story" not only provides historians with valuable insights into the lives of Nero and Sporo, but also serves as a guide for wedding enthusiasts seeking to create unique and historically-inspired wedding experiences. Whether you are planning a lavish celebration or an intimate gathering, this book offers a wealth of knowledge and inspiration to ensure that your special day is steeped in the beauty and intrigue of the past.

Reflecting on the Beauty of Historical Themed Weddings

Historians have always been fascinated by the rich tapestry of human history, and what better way to celebrate love than by incorporating historical elements into a wedding ceremony? In the subchapter titled "Reflecting on the Beauty of Historical Themed Weddings" from the book "The Wedding Between Nero and Sporo: A Historical Love Story," we delve into the captivating world of historical weddings and all the intricate details that make them truly unforgettable.

For those who are captivated by "The Wedding Between Nero and Sporo," this subchapter offers an in-depth exploration of the wedding planning process for historical themed weddings. From meticulously researching and recreating ancient Roman wedding traditions and rituals to finding unique wedding venues that transport guests back in time, this subchapter is a treasure trove of inspiration for couples seeking a truly extraordinary wedding experience.

One aspect that often takes center stage in historical themed weddings is the fashion and attire. This subchapter explores the ancient Roman wedding attire and fashion, highlighting the opulence and elegance that defined this era. From flowing togas to intricate jewelry, every detail is carefully examined to help couples and historians recreate the essence of the Roman Empire in their wedding celebrations.

Of course, no wedding is complete without beautiful memories captured in photographs and videos. This subchapter delves into the world of historical wedding photography and videography, offering tips and tricks for capturing the essence of the past in a modern medium. From choosing the right settings to incorporating historical elements in poses and lighting, this section is a must-read for couples and photographers alike.

Furthermore, this subchapter explores the world of historical wedding favors and decorations, showcasing unique ideas that transport guests to a different time period. From Roman-inspired trinkets to intricate centerpieces, every detail adds to the immersive experience of a historical themed wedding.

Lastly, for those seeking entertainment with a historical twist, this subchapter offers suggestions for wedding reception entertainment. From historical reenactments to live performances inspired by the Roman Empire, there are endless possibilities to create an unforgettable experience that will leave guests in awe.

In conclusion, "Reflecting on the Beauty of Historical Themed Weddings" is a subchapter that celebrates the love for history and the desire to create unique and memorable wedding experiences. From detailed wedding planning to fashion, photography, favors, and entertainment, this subchapter is a comprehensive guide for historians and couples who wish to embark on a journey to the past on their special day.

Acknowledging the Importance of Historical Love Stories in Today's Society

Love stories have always captivated the hearts and minds of people throughout history. They transport us to different eras, cultures, and societies, allowing us to experience the power of love in unique and intriguing ways. In the realm of historical love stories, few tales are as captivating as the wedding between Nero and Sporo.

"The Wedding Between Nero and Sporo: A Historical Love Story" delves deep into the lives of these two individuals, their love for each other, and the challenges they faced in a society that often frowned upon their relationship. This subchapter aims to explore the significance of historical love stories in today's society, particularly for historians and those interested in unique wedding themes and experiences.

For historians, studying historical love stories offers valuable insights into the social, cultural, and political dynamics of a particular era. Through the lens of love, we gain a deeper understanding of the complexities of human relationships, the constraints imposed by society, and the resilience of individuals in overcoming adversity. The wedding between Nero and Sporo provides a fascinating case study of the intersections between power, love, and identity in ancient Rome.

Furthermore, for those interested in historical-themed weddings, the love story of Nero and Sporo serves as an inspiration for creating memorable and unique experiences. From incorporating ancient Roman wedding traditions and rituals to designing wedding attire and fashion inspired by the Roman empire, the possibilities are endless. Imagine exchanging vows in a stunning venue reminiscent of ancient Rome, surrounded by lavish decorations and historical wedding favors.

Moreover, the story of Nero and Sporo also holds relevance for LGBTQ+ historical weddings. In a time when same-sex relationships were not widely accepted, their union challenges societal norms and reminds us of the struggles faced by the LGBTQ+ community throughout history. Their love story serves as a powerful symbol of resilience, love, and the fight for equal rights.

Additionally, the subchapter delves into the realm of historical wedding photography and videography. Imagine capturing the essence of a historical-themed wedding through stunning visuals, recreating the romance and grandeur of Nero and Sporo's union. Furthermore, entertaining guests at the wedding reception with historical reenactments or performances adds a unique twist to the celebration.

In conclusion, historical love stories, such as the wedding between Nero and Sporo, hold immense importance in today's society. They provide historians with valuable insights into the past and offer inspiration for those seeking unique wedding experiences. Whether it is through exploring ancient Roman traditions, LGBTQ+ historical weddings, or capturing the essence through photography and entertainment, these stories continue to captivate and inspire us in the present day.

Encouraging the Preservation and Celebration of Historical Traditions in Weddings.

Encouraging the Preservation and Celebration of Historical Traditions in Weddings

Weddings are not just a celebration of love and commitment between two individuals; they are also an opportunity to honor and preserve the historical traditions that have shaped our society. In this subchapter, we delve into the various ways in which couples can infuse their weddings with historical significance, catering to the interests and passions of historians and enthusiasts alike.

For those fascinated by the captivating love story between Nero and Sporo, this subchapter serves as a guide to planning weddings inspired by their romance. From incorporating ancient Roman wedding rituals and traditions to recreating the opulent Roman empire-inspired wedding themes, couples can transport their guests back in time and immerse them in the grandeur of an ancient love story.

Moreover, we explore the realm of historical reenactment weddings, where couples can bring history to life by reliving significant moments in time. Whether it's a medieval-themed wedding complete with knights and princesses or a Victorian-era soiree with elegant ball gowns and top hats, these unique wedding venues cater to the desires of history enthusiasts who crave an authentic experience.

Additionally, we delve into LGBTQ+ historical weddings, shedding light on the rich history of same-sex unions throughout different cultures and time periods. By celebrating and embracing these stories, couples can honor the struggles and triumphs of the LGBTQ+ community while also crafting a wedding that reflects their own identities.

The subchapter also explores the importance of historical wedding attire and fashion. From ancient Roman togas to Victorian corsets, we guide couples in selecting the perfect attire that encapsulates the spirit of a bygone era. Alongside this, we discuss the significance of historical wedding photography and videography, providing tips on capturing the essence of a historical-themed wedding through visual storytelling.

Furthermore, we offer guidance on selecting historical wedding favors and decorations that reflect the chosen era. Whether it's Roman-inspired pottery or medieval-themed trinkets, these thoughtful details add an extra layer of authenticity to the wedding experience.

Lastly, we delve into the realm of wedding reception entertainment with a historical twist. From lively Renaissance dances to theatrical performances depicting historical events, there are countless ways to keep guests engaged and entertained while also immersing them in the historical context of the wedding.

By encouraging the preservation and celebration of historical traditions in weddings, we create a platform that not only captivates historians but also allows couples to express their love and commitment in a unique and meaningful way. Whether it's through ancient Roman rituals, LGBTQ+ historical narratives, or reenactments of monumental events, these weddings serve as a testament to the enduring power of history in shaping our lives and love stories.